Library Plagiarism Policies

CLIP Note #37

Compiled by

Vera Stepchyshyn
Long Island University
Brooklyn, New York

Robert S. Nelson
Long Island University
Brooklyn, New York

College Library Information Packet Committee
College Libraries Section
Association of College and Research Libraries
A Division of the American Library Association
Chicago 2007

The paper used in this publication meets the minimum requirements of the American National Standard for Information Sciences-Permanence of Paper for Printed Library Materials, ANSI Z39.48-1992.

Library of Congress Cataloging-in-Publication Data

Library plagiarism policies / compiled by Vera Stepchyshyn, Robert S. Nelson.
    p. cm. -- (Clip note ; #37)
  Includes bibliographical references.
  Summary: "Resource for developing policies on the prevention and detection of plagiarism"--Provided by publisher.
  Includes bibliographical references.
  ISBN 978-0-8389-8416-1
  1. Academic libraries--Rules and practice. 2. Plagiarism. 3. Library orientation for college students. 4. Library surveys--United States. I. Stepchyshyn, Vera. II. Nelson, Robert S., 1972-

  Z675.U5L52353 2007
  025.1'977--dc22
                              2007006414

Printed on recycled paper.

Printed in the United States of America.

12 11 10 09 08 07   5 4 3 2 1

Cover design by Jim Lange Design

Table of Contents

Clip Notes Committee

Ann M. Watson, Chair
Denison University Libraries
Denison University
Granville, OH

Susan C. Awe
Parish Memorial Library
University of New Mexico
Albuquerque, NM

Rachel C. Crowley
Bishop Mueller Library
Briar Cliff University
Sioux City, IA

Nancy E. Frazier
E.H. Butler Library
Buffalo State College
Buffalo, NY

Gillian S. Gremmels
Vogel Library
Wartburg College
Waverly, IA

Elizabeth A. Kocevar-Weidinger
Greenwood Library
Longwood University
Farmville, VA

Doreen M. Kopycinski
Library and Technology Services
Lehigh University
Bethlehem, PA

Cherie Alexandra Madarash-Hill
Sims Memorial Library
Southeastern Louisiana University
Hammond, LA

Debbie L. Malone
DeSales University Library
DeSales University
Center Valley, PA

Myrna Joy McCallister
Cunningham Memorial Library
Indiana State University
Terre Haute, IN

William Neal Nelson
Reese Library
Augusta State University
Augusta, GA 30904-2200

Rick Dyson
Missouri Western State University
Library
Missouri Western State University
Saint Joseph, MO

Introduction

OBJECTIVE

With the publication of this book, we hope to provide college libraries, their faculty, their staff, and their administrators with a pragmatic resource for developing policies on the prevention and detection of plagiarism. This study gathered data and documents from small college libraries and presents them for the reader's consideration when examining the issue of student plagiarism and its relationship to the college library. The overall objective of this project is to bring to light the need for libraries to develop policies and procedures that address the prevention and detection of plagiarism.

BACKGROUND

The task of plagiarism prevention and detection is often perceived within the auspices of the college librarian. The college librarian, after all, is an information professional, well versed in web and electronic resource searching, and has the skill-base needed to quickly and effectively retrieve evidence of plagiarism. While the use of the librarian as a plagiarism prevention and detection resource is on the rise, the number of libraries that have formalized, through policy statements or other documents, the responsibilities of librarians is still relatively small and for good reason.

It is easy to state that the library and its librarians should play a role in plagiarism prevention and detection. The information literacy standards set forth by the ACRL clearly note the ethical employment of information as a key trait in an information literate individual. It is more difficult, however, to define what those responsibilities are and where they begin, and even more tenuous to determine where they end. There may be no need for a policy statement on the teaching of proper citation of resources, but there is decidedly a need for a policy statement on the lengths to which a librarian can go on behalf of a faculty member to determine acts of plagiarism.

Librarians and library administrators are presently struggling to create these policies. To that end, this study was conducted to determine what, if anything, is available that may serve as a model for institutions looking to create policies and documents that clearly define the issues for students, faculty, and librarians. The proceeding information should be of interest to any institution investigating this matter.

SURVEY PROCEDURE

In keeping with the guidelines established by the CLIP Notes committee, this survey was drafted, reviewed, and revised according to the committee's recommendations. The decision was made to conduct an exclusively electronic survey. The services of the web-based survey firm, SurveyMonkey, were employed in the creation and delivery of the survey to the participants. Once the instrument was vetted and uploaded to the SurveyMonkey server, it was released via an email database that was able to track participation to the 279 institutions that comprise the CLIP Notes participant database. In addition to the email invitation, a postcard invitation was sent with the URL of the survey prominently displayed.

SURVEY RESULTS

Of the 279 librarians invited to participate, 94 responded to the survey. That is a 34% response rate overall. While a statistically representative sample, the number of respondents was less than expected. This may have been due to the decision to only deliver the survey electronically. Twenty, or 23%, of the 88 respondents who submitted responses to one survey question, stated that their libraries had plagiarism prevention and detection policies. Seventy percent provided web addresses for their plagiarism prevention and detection policies. Of the remaining six respondents who reported their policies were not available online, only one provided a copy of their document.

General Information (Questions 1-12)

The initial question-set sought to collect information about the institutions, the respondents, and to assist in creating a general portrait of the participating libraries. Of the responding libraries, 36% were affiliated with public colleges, 62% were associated with private schools, and 2% classified themselves as "other." Four respondents chose to skip the question.

An examination of the respondents' years at their current libraries and years as professional librarians yields and interesting profile. The average number of years at the current institution was 12, with a range from less than one year to 36 years. Similar ranges and results were tabulated for the question regarding years as a professional librarian. Among the librarians responding, the average number of years in the profession was 20, and one librarian had 45 years of experience. The respondents can thus be classified as seasoned professionals with a fair degree of experience at their current libraries.

The average number of full-time professional librarians in the surveyed institutions was seven. No library reported fewer than two or more than 20 librarians in its current complement of professional staff/faculty. Eighty-three percent of the institutions whose librarians answered the question had a central library administration. The profile of the responding institutions would then be concurrent with the CLIP Notes guidelines.

Policy Information (Questions 13-23)

Only 23% of the respondents claimed to have a policy, position statement, or other document on plagiarism prevention and detection. This is in line with the authors' initial hypothesis that few libraries have formulated official documents that address this issue. Even fewer libraries, only 2% of the total respondents to the question, refer to plagiarism prevention and detection in their mission statements. Given the inherently positive tenor of mission statements and their tendencies to promote the library as a support mechanism for learning, this is an understandable figure.

What is surprising is the seeming lack of outcomes assessment plans for plagiarism prevention and detection efforts. Only 4% of the 84 respondents that chose to answer this question noted that their libraries had outcomes assessment plans for plagiarism prevention and detection. In this age of accountability in academia, it is interesting to see that outcomes assessment of plagiarism prevention and detection work is not more prevalent. This is certainly an area for researchers and policy-makers to address.

Service opportunities and responsibilities of librarians on institutional committees that address the issue of plagiarism were relatively light. Only 33% of the respondents noted that committees exist, and 28% replied that a librarian holds a seat on said committees. While this is not unusual, it does suggest that the forming of campus or university-wide committees to address this issue may need to be explored. The impetus for committees of this type could be generated by the library, thereby ensuring the presence of a librarian on a committee charged with promoting academic integrity on campus.

Of respondents who noted the existence of a plagiarism prevention and detection document, the majority (94%) replied that the college or university's policies on academic integrity influenced or informed their own documents. While institutional policies were readily referenced, the applicable ACRL Information Literacy Competency Standards for Higher Education did not generate as much attention. Thirty-one percent of the respondents noted that their policies or documents referenced or were informed by the national standards. It would be the recommendation of the authors that this trend be examined carefully. The information literacy standards are an important touchstone when dealing with the issue of plagiarism; they should have some impact on the way a library deals with this matter.

The availability and revision of the documents was addressed in questions 20 to 23. A majority (56%) of the respondents reported that their policies were regularly revised, with most policies noted as being revised in the last year. Only 6% of the respondents noted that the policy was never revised. This would indicate that the majority of the documents and policies that do exist are living entities that evolve over time. Sixty-seven percent replied that these policies are available via the Internet and are posted on the library's website. Both electronically accessible and mutable documents are viewed as the most effective. By providing public access to a document that is regularly maintained, libraries are able to demonstrate their attention to this issue and have an easily referable resource.

Librarian Responsibilities/Activities (Questions 24-31)

This section of the survey sought to collect data on what the individual librarian was asked to do with regards to plagiarism prevention and detection. The overall results were, to a degree, surprising, but not wholly unexpected. Of the 82 librarians who responded to the question, 85% replied that they were not responsible for plagiarism prevention and detection as part of their job description or regular duties. However, a small percentage (17%) did note that there was a librarian who had been designated as the official contact for matters regarding plagiarism. This minority listed similar responsibilities, including workshops, library instruction sessions and other outreach efforts. Some are asked "regularly" by faculty to investigate instances of suspected plagiarism. The use of and training in detection tools, such as www.turnitin.com, in three cases fell under the auspices of the librarians. It would then appear that while plagiarism prevention and detection is an issue, only a select group of librarians count it as part of their daily routine. While the number of dedicated "plagiarism librarians" is small, 79% of the respondents noted that they were asked by non-library faculty to detect or research suspected cases of plagiarism. Many (56%) noted that this occurred occasionally, 10% listed it as a frequent occurrence, with the remaining reporting that it rarely happened.

The tools that are employed in these efforts ranged from search-engine queries (44%) to detection software (10%), with citation and bibliography analysis used only 19% of the time. Twenty-seven percent of the respondents employed some combination of the three methods. When asked to elaborate on the methodologies employed when utilizing multiple tools, the following narrative was typical of the 26 responses:

> *A superficial analysis of citations is done to determine which search engines are likely to produce the citations in question. Citations are traced to see if they are even likely available at our library or easily accessed in our area. Questionable sections of the document in question are used to see if there is direct 'lifting' of text (obviously easier if the text is available online). If it appears that the text was reworked rather than 'lifted' (poor paraphrasing), the professor is notified of that fact as well.*

Additional methods included:

While we will run suspected passages through Turnitin.com, we also usually check JSTOR, Muse, Infotrac and Google.

We recently found that a student had plagiarized his paper by copying the entire DVD description in the jewel case. A librarian just tried the DVD case on a hunch. We have found that students took whole passages from books in our collection.

This provides an interesting insight into the creative problem-solving techniques that some librarians will employ to accomplish this task. While tools such as www.turnitin.com are gaining popularity it is important to note that several respondents were unwilling to rely solely on such products' findings.

The most startling result of this inquiry might be the lack of library instruction and information literacy programs that include plagiarism prevention and detection as part of their syllabus or instruction. Only 46% included plagiarism prevention and detection in their library instruction. More than half (54%) replied that it was not included. It is unclear to the authors how, if the ACRL information literacy standards are adhered to, this issue can be excluded when conducting library instruction. The ethical use of information is a primary indicator of information literacy and should be a staple of any library instruction effort.

Incidents and Action (Questions 32-46)

Of interest to the authors was the number of cases detected or reported to the library, the frequency of those actions, as well as what procedures exist with regards to follow-up and reporting. The results of this section could aid in the development of policies and manuals.

Cases of plagiarism were not reported to the library according to most respondents. Only 39% noted that non-library faculty reported cases of plagiarism directly to the library. Whether these cases were reported elsewhere was not explored, but would make for an interesting research project. Eighty-one percent of the 31 respondents who received reported acts state that their libraries receive an average of one and five reports per semester. When asked about what action is taken when cases are reported, the following represents a sample of responses to that question:

The student is failed on the assignment. The faculty member then makes sure that the student knows what plagiarism is. The Academic Dean is consulted for continued plagiarism and the student may be failed on the entire course.

The most common incident report is materials taken from periodicals (scissored [sic] out), and we attempt to recover those materials and charge the perpetrator. We have no academic authority.

Usually one of the librarians is asked to check sources if plagiarism is suspected and if the faculty member has failed to turn up anything in a simple Google search. The librarian reports back to the faculty member the results of their research and the faculty member handles the resolution of the situation.

While non-library faculty often did not report incidents to the library, 92% of the respondents did note that the librarians detect, on average, zero to five cases a semester. The following is a sample of what action the librarians take in these cases:

The library notify [sic] the appropriate department chair.

Librarians discourage plagiarism and encourage students to cite properly, [and] frequently explain when to cite in the context of reference and course-related instruction. If involved in an issue of plagiarism, the librarian would be working with a faculty member who wouuld [sic] determine if an action is to take place. Most departments have procedures, which lead eventually to the Dean of Students, but would most likely be handled by the department itself.

Students detected of plagiarizing are referred to the Student Judiciary's Honor Council.

It should be noted that the legal/judicial process is repeatedly referred to 86% of the respondents. What is of interest is that librarians, although asked to participate in the detection process, rarely (7%) hold seats on such judicial bodies. If librarians were being asked to participate in the detection process, it would stand to reason that they should be invited to participate in the judicial process as well.

The official penalties for confirmed cases of plagiarism fell within standard procedures for colleges. Failure and/or expulsion were common penalties, while one institution noted that students would be asked to write an essay on plagiarism.

Personal/Professional Experiences (Questions 39-47)

Plagiarism seems to be a common occurrence according to the respondents, but few (31%) of the respondents claimed to have directly encountered acts of plagiarism in the library. When plagiarism was encountered, it was primarily cutting and pasting from electronic resources and failure to appropriately document sources. This would signal the need for increased instruction in citation methods as well as exploration of new and existing technologies to mitigate the ability to cut and paste.

Not surprisingly, 95% of the responding librarians noted that their library science courses did not address this issue. While the current library science degree programs may be tackling this matter, these responses serve as a call for workshops and professional development programs. In-service librarians are being asked to perform functions such as plagiarism prevention and detection without adequate training. The library science programs should seize on this opportunity to create certification programs or continuing education classes that would help train librarians in detecting and preventing plagiarism.

The range of opinions on the role of the academic librarian in plagiarism prevention and detection varies widely. While many librarians acknowledged this as an important issue, the respondents, as a group, were concerned about the level of involvement and the actual role librarians should play. The majority noted "education" or "training" as a primary responsibility, but were reticent about becoming "police" or "spies" for the faculty. All said that collaboration was essential.

On the issue of collaboration, approximately three-quarters of the respondents (76%) worked with other (non-library) faculty members to detect plagiarism. This collaboration took many forms with consultations, bibliography analysis, and symposia as the most predominant forms. Websites and awareness events also were mentioned as ways of collaborating with faculty members. When asked to describe their collaborations with faculty members, respondents expressed numerous similarities. Open lines of communication, the acknowledgement of librarians, as experts in this area, and the realization of the need for education were all common.

CONCLUSION

The issue of plagiarism is not new to colleges or college libraries. The advent of new information technologies coupled with an increasingly computer-literate student body has, however, magnified the scope of the problem. It has also brought to light the need for academic and college libraries to address this issue on an institutional level. If librarians are asked to participate in the prevention and detection of plagiarism, then library administrations must begin to wrestle with this problem and begin to create policies that define and govern the level of participation and the actual professional responsibilities of their librarians.

In this litigious society, the security afforded by official and public policies must not be overlooked. It would benefit libraries to begin to draft policies and public documents that can serve as defense against any claims of inappropriate involvement. As this issue grows, the enforcement of expulsion or punitive actions will grow as well. For librarians involved in detecting cases of plagiarism, the need for an officially approved policy is vital to protect them from litigation.

As noted by the respondents, the act of detection is, and should be, a secondary responsibility. The act of prevention must be paramount. The need to educate students in the appropriate and ethical use of information is set forth in the ACRL information literacy standards. It is then the responsibility of libraries to build this mandate into their mission statements, their policies, and even the job descriptions of professional librarians. If the task of prevention is taken seriously, then the necessity for detection should decrease exponentially.

The authors hope that this book, the results of the survey, and the policies provided will help other libraries in tackling this important issue.

Selected Bibliography

Adams, M. "Plagiarism: Finding It and Stopping It." Library Issues: Briefings for Faculty and Administrators 22.6 (Jul 2002): 1-4.

Anderson, Arthur James. "How Do You Manage: A Lesson in Plagiarism 101." Library Journal 119.10 (June 1, 1994): 80-2.

Anderson, Gregory L. "Cyberplagiarism: A Look at the Web Term Paper Sites." College and Research Libraries News 60.5 (May 1999): 371-3, 394.

Auer, Nicole J. and Ellen M. Krupar. "Mouse Click Plagiarism: The role of Technology in Plagiarism and the Librarian's Role in Combating it." Library Trends 49.3 (Winter 2001): 415-32.

Bowman, Vibiana, ed. The Plagiarism Plague: A Resource Guide and CD-ROM Tutorial for Educators and Librarians. New York: Neal-Schuman Publishers, 2004.

Brandt, D. Scott. "Copyright's (Not So) Little Cousin, Plagiarism." Computers in Libraries 22.5 (May 2002): 39-41.

Brine, Alan and Ruth Stubbings. "Plagiarism and the Role of the Library." Library and Information Update 2.12 (Dec 2003): 42-44.

Cast, Melissa. "Plagiarism." Nebraska Library Association Quarterly 34.4 (Winter 2003): 17-24.

Dowd, Steven B. Academic Integrity: A Review and Case Study. Washington, DC: U.S. Dept of Education, Office of Educational Research and Improvement, 1992. [ED349060]

Duggan, Fiona. "The Plagiarism Advisory Service: Promoting Best Practice in Dealing with Plagiarism." Library and Information Research News 27.86 (Summer 2003): 37-42.

Eckert, Janet. "Plagiarism: As Easy as Cut and Paste." The Unabashed Librarian 117 (2000): 11-12.

Ercegovac, Zorana and John V. Richardson, Jr. "Academic Dishonesty, Plagiarism Included, in the Digital Age: A Literature Review." College and Research Libraries 65.4 (July 2004): 301-318.

Fain, Margaret and Peggy Bates. "Cheating 101: Paper Mills and You." 1999. Coastal Carolina University. 16 June 2005 http://www.coastal.edu/library/presentations/papermil.html/

Gresham, John. "Cyber-Plagiarism: Technological and Cultural Background and Suggested Responses." Catholic Library World 73.1 (Sept 2002): 16-19.

Gresham, Keith. "Preventing Plagiarism of the Internet: Teaching Library Researchers How and Why to Cite Electronic Sources." Colorado Libraries 22 (Summer 1996): 48-50.

Hamilton, Denise. "Plagiarism: Librarians Help Provide New Solutions to an Old Problem." Searcher 11.4 (Apr 2003): 26-8.

Hannabuss, Stuart. "Contested Texts: Issues of Plagiarism." Library Management 22.6/7 (2001): 311-18.

Harris, Robert A. The Plagiarism Handbook: Strategies for Preventing, Detecting, and Dealing with Plagiarism. Los Angeles, CA: Pyrczak Publishing, 2001.

Hurlbert, Janel McNeil, Cathleen R. Savidge, and Georgia R. Laudenslager. "Process-Based Assignments: How Promoting Information Literacy Prevents Plagiarism." College and Undergraduate Libraries 10.1 (2003): 39-51.

Jaeger, John. "Plagiarism on the Internet." Christian Librarian 46.2 (2003): 52-4.

Johnson, Anna-Marie. "Web Sites on Plagiarism." Kentucky Libraries 66.3 (Summer 2002): 16.

Lampert, Lynn D. "Integrating Discipline Based Anti-Plagiarism Instruction in to the Information Literacy Curriculum." Reference Services Review 32.4 (2004): 347-55.

Liddell, Jean. "A Comprehensive Definition of Plagiarism." Community and Junior College Libraries 11.3 (2003): 43-52.

Liles, Jeffrey A. and Michael E. Rozalski. "It's a Matter of Style: A Style Manual Workshop for Preventing Plagiarism." College and Undergraduate Libraries 11.2 (2004): 91-101.

Mounce, Michael. "Plagiarism Detection and Prevention: Creating Online Guides for Faculty and Students." Mississippi Libraries 68.3 (Fall 2004): 67-70.

Pennsylvania. Office of Commonwealth Libraries. But I Changed the Words: Educating the Cut and Paste Generation. Harrisburg, PA: Pennsylvania Department of Education, 2002.

Simmonds, Patience. "Plagiarism and Cyber-Plagiarism: A Guide to Selected Resources on the Web." College and Research Libraries News 64.6 (June 2003): 385-9.

Smith, C. Brian. "Fighting Cyberplagiarism." Library Journal Net Connect (Summer 2003): 22-3.

Stebelman, Scott. Cybercheating: Dishonesty Goes Digital. American Libraries 29.8 (Sept 1998): 48-50.

Todaro, Julie Beth. "Nothing But Net." Community and Junior College Libraries 12.1 (2004): 91-97.

Trinchera, Tom. "Cut and Paste Plagiarism: What It Is and What to Do About It." Community and Junior College Libraries 10.3 (2001): 5-9.

Willems, Harry. "Plagiarism – The Library Connection." The Unabashed Librarian 124 (2002): 20-1.

Willis, Dottie J. "High Tech Cheating: Plagiarism and the Internet." <u>Kentucky Libraries</u> 65.4 (Fall 2001): 28-30.

Wood, Gail. "Academic Original Sin: Plagiarism, the Internet, and Librarians." <u>Journal of Academic Librarianship</u> 30.3 (May 2004): 237-42.

CLIP Note Survey Results

Survey: Plagiarism Detection and Prevention

PERSONAL INFORMATION (Questions 1 – 7)

1. **Name:**   34% response rate   (94 responses)

2. **Title:**   (94 responses)

Library Director/Head/Dean/University Librarian	(55)
Reference/Instruction/Public Services Librarian	(13)
Asst. Director/Associate Dean/V.P. Library/ies	(6)
Head of Reference/Public Services	(5)
Electronic Resources/Information Tech. Librarian	(4)
Tech. Serv. Librarian (Cat./Acq./Serials)	(4)
Instruction/Information Lit. Librarian/Coordinator	(3)
Assistant Director Public Services	(1)
Assistant	(1)
Assistant Director of Personnel & Planning	(1)
Web Developer	(1)

3. **Years at Current Institution:**   (70 responses)

          RANGE: 6 Months – 36 Years
          AVERAGE: 12 Years

4. **Years as a Professional Librarian:**   (71 responses)

          RANGE: Less than 1 Year – 45 Years
          AVERAGE: 20 Years

5. **Can we contact you regarding your responses to this survey?**

                                                                   (94 responses)

          Yes: 90%   (85)
          No: 10%   (10)

6. **E-mail Address:**   (82 responses)

7. **Phone Number:**   (79 responses)

INSTITUTION INFORMATION (Questions 8 – 12)

8. **College/University Name:**   (90 responses)

9. **What type of institution does your library belong to?**   (90 responses)

          Public: 36%   (32)
          Private: 62%   (56)
          Other: 2%   (2)

10. **How many Full-Time Equivalent (FTE) students are currently enrolled in your institution?** (90 responses)

RANGE: 720 – 26,000
AVERAGE: 3509

11. **How many Full-Time Professional Librarians does your library employ?** (88 responses)

RANGE: 2 – 20
AVERAGE: 7

12. **Is there a central library administration?** (83 responses)

Yes: 83% (69)
No: 17% (14)

POLICY (Questions 13 – 23)

13. **Does your library have a policy, position statement, or other document on plagiarism prevention and detection?** (88 responses)

Yes: 23% (20)
No: 77% (68)

14. **Is plagiarism prevention and detection referenced in the library's mission statement?** (84 responses)

Yes: 2% (2)
No: 98% (82)

15. **Is there an outcomes assessment plan for plagiarism prevention and detection efforts for the library?** (84 responses)

Yes: 4% (3)
No: 96% (81)

16. **Is there a college or university-wide committee formed to address the issue of plagiarism?** (84 responses)

Yes: 33% (28)
No: 67% (56)

17. **If there is a committee to address plagiarism prevention and detection, does a librarian hold a seat on that committee?** (47 responses)

Yes: 28% (13)
No: 72% (34)

18. **Is the library's plagiarism policy informed by the college or university's policy?**

(16 responses)

Yes:	94%	(15)
No:	6%	(1)

19. **Is the policy informed by or does it reference the applicable ACRL Information Literacy Standards?**

(16 responses)

Yes:	31%	(5)
No:	69%	(11)

20. **How often is the library's plagiarism policy reviewed and revised?**

(16 responses)

Regularly:	56%	(9)
Rarely:	38%	(6)
Never:	6%	(1)

21. **If the policy is reviewed and revised, please provide us with the date of the last revision.**

(11 responses)

2005:	27%	(3)
2004:	55%	(6)
2003:	9%	(1)
1999:	9%	(1)

22. **Is the policy posted on the library's website?**

(15 responses)

Yes:	67%	(11)
No:	33%	(4)

23. **If you answered YES to Question 22, please provide us with the web address.**

(11 responses)

LIBRARIAN RESPONSIBILITIES/ACTIVITIES (Questions 24 – 31)

24. **Are the professional librarians responsible for plagiarism prevention and detection?**

(82 responses)

Yes:	15%	(12)
No:	85%	(70)

25. **Is there a librarian designated as an official contact for plagiarism detection?**

(82 responses)

Yes:	17%	(14)
No:	83%	(68)

26. **If you answered YES to Question 25, please describe their responsibilities.**

(17 responses)

- *Asked by faculty to assist in detecting plagiarism in particular student papers.*

- *Liaison work with teaching faculty to detect plagiarism, conduct workshops, send out information on campus list, etc.*
- *Informal and depends on what each faculty member faced by a suspicious paper chooses to do.*
- *Director of Library Services receives student papers that are suspicious and forwards them to Turnitin for analysis.*
- *Work with faculty on revisions of the policy and develop teaching tools to help students better understand what plagiarism is.*
- *On our campus the registrar is the contact person.*
- *Answer questions on copyright.*
- *Librarians teach other faculty Turnitin.*

27. **Are librarians asked by other (non-library) faculty members to research or detect suspected cases of plagiarism?** (82 responses)

        Yes: 79%   (65)
        No: 21%   (17)

28. **If they are asked to research or detect suspected cases of plagiarism, how often are they asked to perform these functions?** (68 responses)

        Frequently: 10%   (7)
        Occasionally: 56%   (38)
        Rarely: 34%   (23)

29. **What methods of research or detection are employed?** (68 responses)

        Search-engine queries: 44%   (30)
        Detection Software (i.e. Turnitin): 10%   (7)
        Citation and Bibliography analysis: 19%   (13)
        All of the above: 27%   (18)

30. **If a combination of research and detection methods is used, please describe the methodologies.** (29 responses)

- *While we will run suspected passages through Turnitin, we also usually check JSTOR, Muse, Infotrac and Google.*
- *Library databases, search engines, review monographs and reference materials.*
- *We use both search engine queries and citation/bibliography analysis, but not detection software. I believe there are several individual departments of the University that employ plagiarism detection software.*
- *Turnitin is available on campus but is not managed by the Library.*
- *Questionable sections of the document in question are used to see if there is direct 'lifting' of text (obviously easier if the text is available online). If it appears that the text was reworked rather than 'lifted' (poor paraphrasing), the professor is notified of that fact as well.*
- *We recently found that a student had plagiarized his paper by copying the entire DVD description in the jewel case. A librarian just tried the DVD case on a hunch.*
- *Librarians are turned to as a last resort – faculty is capable of doing the usual search-engine queries, as are the administrators who handle honor code cases.*

We help in any way, usually by providing copies of articles or book segments, in problem cases.

- *Just because we are asked doesn't mean we'll do it. Our job is to help teach about good citation practice, not to police plagiarism.*
- *Informed hit and miss research.*
- *Library Director maintains a web page of informational web sites on plagiarism.*

31. Is plagiarism prevention and detection a part of your library instruction program or library instruction syllabus? (82 responses)

Yes: 46% (38)
No: 54% (44)

INCIDENTS AND ACTION (Questions 32 – 38)

32. Are cases of plagiarism reported to the library by other (non-library) faculty?
(82 responses)

Yes: 39% (32)
No: 61% (50)

33. How many incidents of plagiarism, on average, are reported to the library in a semester? (31 responses)

1 – 5:	81%	(25)
6 – 10:	13%	(4)
11 – 20:	6%	(2)
20 + :	0%	(0)

What, if any, action is taken?

- *This is not an official reporting policy or procedure (e.g. we aren't the college plagiarism police nor do we hold any authority in such cases, we're simply a resource to assist faculty in this area). Plagiarism is addressed in our college honor code for students. If a student is found to have committed plagiarism, a faculty member has the option of bringing that student before the campus judicial board, which is comprised of students, the dean of students, and two faculty representatives (one male, one female).*
- *The faculty member has the option of reporting the plagiarism to the Academic Dean who keeps a file and may dismiss if a number of incidents are reported for the same students. Faculty members most often just give the student an 'F' for the assignment.*
- *This is the responsibility of the Committee on Academic Integrity.*
- *The Director of Library Services alerts the appropriate professor.*
- *The College policy is explained, (college catalog) and the faculty member is asked if they need assistance in detection.*
- *Professors take action on a case-by-case basis. For first offense generally the paper gets a failing grade. Repeat offenders will fail the entire course or be expelled from school.*

- *A librarian investigates the suspected plagiarism. If the librarian can verify that plagiarism has occurred, the librarian supplies the evidence to the instructor, and is available to confront the student along with the instructor.*

34. **On average, how many incidents of plagiarism does the library detect in a semester?** (49 responses)

0 – 5:	92%	(45)
6 – 10:	6%	(3)
11 – 20:	0%	(0)
20 + :	2%	(1)

35. **Please describe what actions, if any, are taken when plagiarism is detected.** (26 responses)

- *We do not do not actually detect the plagiarism. We are only involved if a faculty member asks for assistance when they suspect plagiarism. For the College, plagiarism is an honor code violation, which sends the suspected student to the honor court for trial.*
- *When requested by a faculty member to look for plagiarism and plagiarism is detected, the faculty member is informed. The library is not notified what action the faculty member takes.*
- *Librarians work with faculty to detect plagiarism. It is the faculty's responsibility to take appropriate action, which may include involving the Vice President of Academic Affairs.*
- *Grade penalty*
- *Plagiarism cases are not reported to the library. They are reported to the Associate Academic Dean. The library provides plagiarism detection as a reference service to faculty.*
- *The professor will probably fail the student.*
- *Suspected students are referred to the Student Judiciary's Honor Council.*
- *It's a faculty-student-administration issue. The library does not get involved.*
- *This is not a library responsibility but left to the individual faculty to report to the appropriate committee per school policy.*
- *Handled by classroom faculty -- actions depend upon divisional standards.*
- *Provost is sometimes involved depending on the action of the instructor.*
- *Suspected students are sent to the Committee on Academic Integrity for a hearing. Disciplinary action is undertaken as appropriate for the infraction.*
- *Faculty member involved pursues the matter with Academic Affairs office.*
- *The library notifies the appropriate department chair.*
- *We work with faculty members, and they take action. There is an honor code policy. If involved in an issue of plagiarism, the librarian would be working with a faculty member who would determine if an action is to take place. Most departments have procedures, which lead eventually to the Dean of Students, but would most likely be handled by the department itself.*

36. **Is there a legal/judicial process for alleged cases of plagiarism at your college or university?** (49 responses)

Yes:	86%	(42)
No:	14%	(7)

37. **Are librarians asked to participate?** (41 responses)

Yes: 7% (3)
No: 93% (38)

38. **What, if any, are the official penalties for confirmed cases of plagiarism?**
(36 responses)

- *Sanctions may include a grade of 'F' for the course work, academic probation, and dismissal from the program and/or dismissal from the university.*
- *Students go before Student Court for an Honor Code violation if they are suspected. If they are convicted the punishment is suspension or expulsion and they receive an 'F' in the course.*
- *Students are required to write an essay about plagiarism; there also may be some grade penalty.*
- *All depends on the case.*
- *According to the College Catalog the penalties for substantiated dishonesty are: 1. Failure of the course or 2. Failure in the paper, test, etc. or 3. Requirement that the work be redone with a suitably substituted assignment. In all cases, the penalty should reflect how seriously the instructor recognizes academic honesty.*
- *1a.. Oral reprimand by instructor 1b. Written reprimand only to student, or 1c. Assignment to be rewritten and judged on merit 2. Disciplinary Sanction (after confirmed academic misconduct) a. conference with student b. report filed*
- *One of the following, depending upon the nature of the course (freshman vs. advanced), severity of the plagiarism, and any pattern of prior incidents: a. reprimand/warning b. assignment of additional work c. lowering grade by one or more grade steps d. re-examination e. lowering grade to zero credit for specific assignment f. assigning grade of F in course (failed) g. dismissal of student from the college, either with possibility of re-admission or without.*
- *In most circumstances, grading is the prerogative of the faculty. However, in cases brought before the Honor Board, all parties are obligated to accept the decision resulting from Honor Board procedure. More severe penalties than a faculty member may assess individually (Penalty F, non-implemented suspension, suspension, expulsion) are the responsibility of the College as a whole, and decisions involving such penalties require the participation of the faculty, the students, and the administration.*
- *If guilty, penalties range from failure to suspension. All those found guilty must attend sessions taught by reference librarian on proper use of sources.*
- *Cases are usually resolved informally between the student and faculty.*
- *Librarians are not officially asked to participate in cases being heard by the Committee on Academic Integrity. However, egregious cases are turned over to the Office of Academic Affairs with the recommendation that the student be placed on leave or expelled. The Library Director participates in the Academic Affairs Officers group. (The group is composed of the College Provost, associate provosts, the registrar, an academic counselor, and the Library Director.) Which is to say, the Library Director has a strong voice in plagiarism cases requiring disciplinary action.*
- *There are 6 pages on this in the Student Handbook.*
- *The faculty member can have a written record of the sequence of events placed in the student's permanent record with a copy to the student.*

PERSONAL/PROFESSIONAL EXPERIENCES (Questions 39 – 47)

39.   **Have you ever, directly, encountered acts of plagiarism in the library?**

(81 responses)

Yes: 31%   (25)
No: 69%   (56)

40.   **Please check the answers that best describe the types of plagiarism you have encountered.**

(25 responses)

Cut and paste from website or electronic article	76%	(19)
Creating a bibliography for a paper that has already been written	28%	(7)
Paper mills or Pay-Per Paper site access	28%	(7)
Failure to appropriately document the source of a quote	64%	(16)
Other (please specify)	28%	(7)

41.   **Did any courses in your library science degree address the issue of plagiarism prevention and detection?**

(79 responses)

Yes: 5%   (4)
No: 95%   (75)

42.   **What is your personal opinion on plagiarism prevention and detection as a responsibility of the academic librarian?**

(66 responses)

- *The responsibility has to be shared with the faculty and the students: faculty has to set clear expectations and students have to know that faculty and librarians can and will track down plagiarism. There needs to be consequences as well.*
- *I see the librarian's role as one of prevention. With our help, the number of cases of accidental plagiarism should decrease. I would not want to see librarians in the role of Plagiarism Police: students would feel even less comfortable asking for assistance and it would drive them further toward the belief that they can get everything they need from the Internet.*
- *This should be a concern of all of us who work in academe - librarians, classroom faculty, administration, and students. We have a responsibility to educate students on not only what constitutes plagiarism and how to avoid doing it, but also why this should be considered a 'big deal.' In other words, we should not only address the technical aspects of the issue but also the ethical ones.*
- *Academic librarians have no responsibility whatsoever for preventing plagiarism: faculty should inform students of what constitutes plagiarism; it is the student's responsibility to submit original work. Librarians and faculty members cannot be held responsible for students' behavior.*
- *Librarians are personally helpful/useful in searching for instances of plagiarism in documents already identified as potentially plagiarized by the instructor. However, librarians are not babysitters, and cannot be expected to spy on students or make assumptions about how items are being used (or credited) based on casual observation.*
- *This is an excellent area around which to form a collaborative working relationship with classroom faculty.*

- *Librarians have a role in the investigation of possible cases of plagiarism. Our broad research skills suit us well in this role.*
- *It is the responsibility of the instructor to make assignments that decrease the possibility of plagiarism and to scrutinize written work. I don't see prevention or detection as being the responsibility of librarians, other than indirectly through instruction classes.*
- *Plagiarism is not part of our instruction program because the topic is part of the instruction by First Year Seminar and English Composition faculty.*
- *We are fortunate to have relatively few cases on our campus. However, I do believe all educators, including academic librarians, have a responsibility to prevent and detect plagiarism. We have a required first year experience class, which includes extensive discussion of plagiarism. This course, which is only two years old, has seemed to dramatically increase student awareness of plagiarism. Perhaps this is one reason we have so few cases.*
- *Like other aspects of the university, the role of the library in plagiarism is to act as an information conduit. We have created a Plagiarism website, with tutorials, web links, and other information. These are readily available to the university population and they address specifically the university's plagiarism policies.*
- *Puts us in a tricky position since we are here to service students and want them to feel comfortable coming to us with questions. We try to emphasize that students' library records are confidential and are NOT used when plagiarism is investigated. We ask faculty to delete students' names from suspected papers that we investigate.*
- *Hardly seems that the library is the appropriate authority. We don't see the end products.*
- *In the course of assisting students librarians should be sure students are aware of citation requirements when using electronic and traditional sources.*
- *We address prevention as part of faculty training and are willing to include an explanation of what plagiarism is in a BI class. We do not involve ourselves in detection, although we are willing to give advice.*
- *Preventing plagiarism by teaching students how to identify and avoid it should be part of the information literacy curriculum, as it addresses ACRL Information Literacy Competency Standard for Higher Education #5: 'An information literate individual is able to understand the economic, legal, and social issues surrounding the use of information, and access and use information ethically and legally.'*

43. **Have you worked with other (non-library) faculty members to detect plagiarism?** (79 responses)

        Yes: 76%   (60)
        No: 24%   (19)

44. **Please choose the answer that best describes how you have collaborated with other (non-library) faculty members on the issue of plagiarism.** (65 responses)

	Formal	Informal	Both	Other	Response Total
Consultations and discussions	8% (5)	52% (33)	38% (24)	2% (1)	(63)
Bibliography analysis	11% (5)	64% (28)	23% (10)	2% (1)	(44)
Research project design assistance	27% (7)	42% (11)	23% (6)	8% (2)	(26)
Campus-wide, university-wide, or other symposia	52% (22)	19% (8)	14% (6)	14% (6)	(42)

45.   **If you have answered OTHER, please describe what form of collaboration you participated in.**   (5 responses)

- *We're planning a brief summer workshop on plagiarism in the library: we'll be looking at the library website and discussing what we can do to help faculty address the plagiarism problem.*
- *Planning an awareness event for first year student orientation next fall.*
- *Faculty workshops; Website with information for faculty; Proposed panel discussion on cheating; Handouts on effective research assignments.*
- *Have given a presentation on Turn-it-in and on the issue of plagiarism.*

46.   **If you have worked with other (non-library) faculty members, please describe that experience.**   (42 responses)

- *A few years ago we did a workshop as part of the faculty Development Day on plagiarism detection. On occasions at the request of faculty members our library instruction sessions include proper citation and avoidance of plagiarism.*
- *Faculty member suspects plagiarism and contacts us for help. They provide the text (or image, etc) and we try to locate the original source.*
- *Have served - and do serve - on committees related to honor codes and to academic integrity. Currently chair a committee looking at campus-wide citation software to support students and faculty in their citation efforts. I also research plagiarism software such as Turnitin but our campus did not elect to purchase.*
- *Our library has provided workshop presentations to faculty on how to handle plagiarism.*
- *Before we signed up with Turnitin I used to show professors how to do advanced searches on Google to determine if students were plagiarizing. Now I accept papers from professors who suspect their students have plagiarized and submit them to Turnitin.*
- *I (Director) presented a workshop with the Teaching and Learning Center of the College. It is sponsored by the VPAA and is faculty (teaching) run. There is a web site that is maintained by the library director.*
- *Faculty seems pleased to have expert assistance in trying to locate plagiarized sources.*
- *Usually the reference librarians aid faculty with plagiarism detection, though increasingly the systems librarian does so. I conducted a plagiarism seminar for the entire campus some years ago.*

- *Most of my work in detecting plagiarism happened long ago when I was a reference librarian. I've had no interaction at that level since becoming director nine years ago. I was on a panel two years ago, sponsored by our teaching center, which addressed various aspects of plagiarism.*
- *I have actively lobbied for a commercial program to be put in place.*
- *I find too many non-library faculty members interested more in detection rather than prevention – and they would like to palm off this task on librarians. As director, I have refused to become a detection mill for the faculty. If they come to the library for help, they must be part of the process. We explain how to detect the plagiarism, but they must do the work. New technologies require new ways of teaching research. The same faculty members visit time after time, refusing to change their teaching methods (i.e., pick a topic and write a paper).*
- *Helped design library instruction sessions and outreach programs that address academic honesty. Librarian serving on campus-wide committee that is discussing the possibility of creating an honor code.*
- *Helped nursing faculty create assignments, distributed resources (academic honesty quiz samples, sample case studies), was invited to observe and comment on a philosophy class role play plagiarism court, have assisted individual faculty with suspected plagiarism research, advised the provost's academic policy committee on revising the college policy.*
- *Was a member of a panel on plagiarism at the NY State Sociological Association Annual Convention.*
- *Worked with Instruction and Research Technology (academic computing support) on issues related to plagiarism*

47. **Please add any additional comments that you feel may aid us in our efforts to develop a better understanding of this issue.** (23 responses)

- *Some faculty wondered if we should get a site license to a service such as Turnitin. I'm conflicted about it, since I don't like the model they set forth of all students turning in papers for a professor through the site: says to me 'Prove you are innocent.' I do like to use the service when plagiarism is suspected, and the tool is used to verify that suspicion.*
- *Academic integrity is the issue that needs to be discussed. If students are involved in the creation of a policy/document the more committed they will be to the ethical standard.*
- *The only written statement currently at our institution is our student Honor Code, which is rather general and doesn't specifically address plagiarism, but does address general academic honesty.*
- *We are using Searchpath tutorial, which touches on the issue. We are also exploring other web sites and materials that we can offer to faculty to use in their classes.*
- *At our college the English faculty accept the role of addressing plagiarism prevention with every freshman. It is also discussed in our college-wide orientation seminar.*
- *Our faculty members often have definitions, which differ to some extent from the one in the Student Handbook or they may not even know we have a definition in the Student Handbook. We must begin to clear up the confusion on this subject from the top down so that the students have a clear understanding of what we are talking about when we speak on plagiarism.*

- *Each campus is different … I think more and more faculty on our campus are finally acknowledging that it is a problem. We have a rather severe penalty system put in place for cheating/plagiarism in the classroom setting. I am concerned that it has the potential to be unevenly and unfairly enforced.*
- *Many of our librarians complain that students caught 'cutting and pasting' in the library respond with, 'my teacher doesn't care.' Librarians have NO AUTHORITY and the sad fact is that we have instructors who do not care or who believe that detection and penalty, rather than prevention, is the answer.*
- *Librarians here have had a major role in helping the college arrive at a plagiarism policy. We also provide links to a variety of websites about plagiarism.*
- *The ideal is for faculty to design assignments that defeat, as much as possible, the blatant plagiarism we see too much of today. In addition, I think there needs to be a redefinition of what plagiarism is in a communication environment of ubiquitous borrowing/sharing of ideas.*
- *We do not currently have librarians serving on the academic honesty judicial board, but librarians have chaired it in the past.*
- *Our plagiarism policies are created by each of the schools in the University, and are specific to the types of work done in those schools.*
- *Our library does not have a separate policy on academic integrity, as we work together with our administrative and academic colleagues to enforce the college policy. After this survey I now wonder if a policy/statement on the role of the library would be helpful.*
- *I do have a concern over a conflict between privacy/confidentiality issues with the student as client, and being the cop on the beat. Do these issues disappear in suspected cases of plagiarism?*
- *The vast majority of students need positive guidance. They are often confused about paraphrasing, about how to express their original ideas - these things are normal and provide a learning opportunity especially at the reference desk.*

Plagiarism Policies

This document was approved by the Faculty on April 6, 1987, for circulation to all students in Bates College.

Bates College does not discriminate on the basis of race, color, national or ethnic origin, religion, sex, sexual orientation, marital or parental status, age, or handicap, in the recruitment and admission of its students, in the administration of its educational policies and programs, or in the recruitment and employment of its faculty and staff.

9/93

Contents

- **Statement of Policy on Plagiarism**
- **Plagiarism**
  - Definition
  - Reasons for Citing Sources
  - What to Cite
- **Proper Citation**
  - General
  - Direct Quotation
  - Paraphrase
  - Information or Ideas
  - Illustrations, Graphs, or Tables
  - Example of Proper and Improper Use of a Source
  - Taking Notes
  - Bibliographic Entries
- **Style Guides**
  - Absence of a Universal Standard
  - Use of Style Manuals
  - Department Recommendations
- **Two Common Methods of Citation**
  - Modified Chicago Style
    - General
    - Footnotes in General
    - Footnotes: First Reference (Books)
    - Footnotes: First Reference (Journal Articles)

Statement of Policy on Plagiarism

Adopted by the Faculty in April 1975

1. Intellectual honesty is fundamental to scholarship. Accordingly, the College views plagiarism or cheating of any kind in academic work as among the most serious offenses that a student can commit.

2. Plagiarism occurs when one presents work which is taken from another person who is not given due credit. ALL STUDENTS WILL BE HELD RESPONSIBLE FOR CAREFULLY READING AND FOLLOWING THE DOCUMENT PROVIDED BY THE COLLEGE, which defines plagiarism and discusses in detail the proper and improper uses of source material. Students who are uncertain in any specific situation as to whether plagiarism may be involved should discuss the matter with their instructor.

3. In order to insure equal and fair treatment for all students, instructors are expected to report to the Dean of Students any cases of plagiarism where there appears to be an intent to deceive, as well as cheating of any kind in student work. Absence of any obvious attempt on the student's part to acknowledge the original source will be taken

as prima facie evidence of such an intent to deceive. If the evidence warrants, the case will then be brought before the Committee on Student Conduct for a hearing.

4. In instances involving questionable or faulty use of source material where culpable motives are not involved, the instructor should warn and advise the student. At the beginning of each semester the instructor should discuss potential problems in the area of plagiarism as they apply to the particular course involved.

Part I: Plagiarism

A. Definition

There are many forms of academic dishonesty. Here we are concerned especially with plagiarism. Plagiarism is the representation of another person's words, ideas, or information as if they were one's own. You may use another person's words, ideas, or information, but to do so without acknowledgment constitutes plagiarism. This applies to both oral and written work.

B. Reasons for Citing Sources

The fundamental reason for citing sources is intellectual honesty. You are guilty of plagiarism if you do not cite your sources.

Citing your sources can also be helpful to you and your reader.

1. You are providing information that your reader may use in seeking further knowledge on your topic, or on a subtopic or peripheral topic that you have treated only briefly.
2. You are providing a means whereby another person may verify the accuracy of your use of sources.
3. Careful citation helps you to know when you do have a new idea, or whether you have achieved a meaningful synthesis of other people's ideas.
4. The same idea might have occurred independently to others. By citing your sources you show how you arrived at it.

C. What to Cite

Although it is impossible to list all possible circumstances, the following illustrate the range to which the principle applies. You may describe Einstein's theory of relativity, but if you present it as your theory you are guilty of plagiarism. You may summarize a Supreme Court opinion in your own words, but if you incorporate the language of the original without indicating that you are doing so, you are guilty of plagiarism. Copying from someone else's paper during an examination is plagiarism. The submission of a term paper purchased from or prepared by someone else also constitutes plagiarism.

Acknowledgment should be made not only for theories, interpretations, ideas, and language adopted from other sources, but also for nonverbal material such as artistic and musical works, illustrations, charts, and experiments. Indicate the sources of data, whether from reference works, computer data files, or your own efforts.

Acknowledge specific detailed assistance from friends, instructors, or others. On collaborative projects, indicate who contributed which portions of the endeavor. Copying another person's lab report or running off a duplicate listing of a computer homework assignment is plagiarism. A student who wishes to submit work for credit in more than one course should consult with the instructor(s) in advance.

Beliefs so widely held as to defy citation and information (such as birth and death dates) obtainable from any of a number of authoritative sources are considered "common knowledge" and need not be cited. Also, phraseology in common use, such as "knowledge is power" (Bacon) or "military-industrial complex" (Eisenhower), may be duplicated without acknowledgment.

It is safer to acknowledge than not to acknowledge. Always supply a reference if you are in doubt; even a crude reference is better than none at all.

Part II: Proper Citation

A. General

Perhaps the most serious form of plagiarism is failure to acknowledge the source of a direct quotation or paraphrase. Language, ideas, or information taken from others should be acknowledged at an appropriate point within the text. *The mere inclusion of a source in the bibliography of a paper does not avoid plagiarism.*

B. Direct Quotation

Quoted matter, from any source, should be distinctly set apart from other text in order to indicate that the language is not your own. Quotation marks are customarily used to mark the beginning and end of the quotation. In typewritten work, long quotations may be set apart by indenting and by single-spacing instead of double-spacing; when this is done, quotation marks are not used.

Be careful not to alter any quoted language without acknowledging that you have done so. Your own remarks inserted into a quotation should be set apart from the quoted material. This is ordinarily done by enclosing them in square brackets. The phrase "emphasis mine" or "emphasis supplied" indicates that you have supplied underlining or other emphasis not found in the original. If a quotation is too long, you may wish to omit parts of it by using an ellipsis, a string of three periods (four at the end of a sentence), to indicate the words omitted.

In some fields the source of a quotation is acknowledged very specifically, as by a page reference; but in all cases the source of a quotation must be acknowledged.

C. Paraphrase

It is not true that only direct quotations must be acknowledged. Failure to acknowledge the source of an indirect quotation, or paraphrase, is also a form of plagiarism. The writer of a paraphrase must acknowledge that it is a paraphrase and must identify the source. If the paraphrase contains phrases from the original source, those phrases must be acknowledged by quotation marks. If your sentence structure, your narrative, or the sequence or logic of your discussion is taken from your source, this fact should be acknowledged. The meaning of the original language must not be distorted in a paraphrase.

D. Information or Ideas

Credit should be given to the source of information or ideas not your own. You should name the articles, books, and other sources you have used in preparing your paper, and give detailed credit (e.g., page or chapter reference) for information and ideas that come from one particular place within the source.

E. Illustrations, Graphs, and Tables
If illustrations, graphs, or tables are photocopied from a source, that source should be acknowledged precisely, e.g., by page or figure number.

If a figure or a table is redrawn or otherwise altered, you should acknowledge the source and indicate the extent to which it was used, as in the following examples:

> From Smith. [Implies minimal alteration.]
> After Smith.
> Modified after Smith.
> Data from Smith and from Jones.

Some writers insert the year in parentheses following the name, thus: After Smith (1960).

F. Example of Proper and Improper Use of a Source
The following passage, relating to the plight of Sioux Indians after 1876, is taken from a book by Helen Hunt Jackson:

> Contrast the condition into which all these friendly Indians are suddenly plunged now, with their condition only two years previous: martial law now in force on all their reservations; themselves in danger of starvation, and constantly exposed to the influence of emissaries from their friends and relations, urging them to join in fighting this treacherous government that had kept faith with nobody-neither with friend nor with foe....

Below are four examples of how the above passage might be used in a term paper. Writer A has committed blatant plagiarism, omitting any form of acknowledgment. Writer B does provide a footnote, but is guilty of plagiarism nevertheless: some direct language quoted by writer B goes unacknowledged, and there is no indication of paraphrase; the footnote is a misleading and inadequate acknowledgment, because it seems to pertain to the final quoted phrase only. Of these examples, only writers C and D have used the source correctly.

Writer A (Plagiarism)
Only two years later, all these friendly Sioux were suddenly plunged into new conditions, including starvation, martial law on all their reservations, and constant urging by their friends and relations to join in warfare against a treacherous government that had kept faith with neither friend nor foe.

Writer B (Plagiarism)
The Sioux were now on the verge of starvation. Martial law was now in force on all their reservations. Emissaries from their friends and relations urged them to join in the fighting against the Federal Government - a "treacherous government that had kept faith with neither friend nor foe."

Writer C (Proper use of source material)
The conditions on Sioux reservations were far worse than they had been before. Jackson writes that "martial law [was] now in force on all their reservations," that the Indians were "in danger of starvation," and that "emissaries from their friends and relations" constantly goaded them "to join in fighting this treacherous government that had kept faith...neither with friend nor with foe."[i]

Writer D (Proper use of souce material)
Conditions on the Sioux reservations had deteriorated seriously within that two year period. Food shortages were severe; the reservations were under martial law; and there was constant pressure to join friends and relations in armed rebellion against the government.[i]

G. Taking Notes
Plagiarism may arise through lack of care in taking notes.

When you are doing research, record the names of the sources from which you are deriving words, ideas, or information; you should usually record the page number or other specific reference to the place from which each piece of material is taken. In your notes, be certain to distinguish between direct quotations, paraphrases, general summaries, and your own comments. If you copy directly from the source, indicate (for example, with quotation marks) that what you have copied is a direct quotation, and should be designated as such if you reproduce this language in your own paper.

You can avoid a great deal of trouble if you are precise about such matters when you do your research in the first place, rather than trying - perhaps unsuccessfully - to find your sources at the last minute. Similarly, it is much easier to take down the full bibliographical data on a source as soon as you begin to use a source rather than going through all of your sources an extra time in order to compile a bibliography.

H. Bibliographic Entries
With some exceptions, most forms of scholarly writing include at the end a list of references. Such a list is commonly called the bibliography; it may include works that have strongly influenced your thinking, even if they are not cited in the text. If a bibliography is restricted to works cited in the text, it might better be titled "References" or "Literature Cited."

Regardless of the format followed, certain information is usually included. For books: author, title, publisher, place of publication, and date of publication; when appropriate, the edition, volume number, or number of volumes. For journal articles: author, title, and inclusive page numbers of the article, journal name, volume number, and year of issue. In citing unpublished material, give as much information as you believe your reader would need in order to find and consult your original source.

---

[i] Helen Hunt Jackson, *A Century of Dishonor, a Sketch of the United States Government's Dealings with Some of the Indian Tribes* (New York: Harper & Bros., 1881), p. 178.

Part III: Style Guides

A. Absence of a Universal Standard

No standard format has earned anything approaching universal acceptance, for different standards are often employed in different fields.

B. Use of Style Manuals

Detailed instructions for citing sources are contained in published style manuals. Generally useful manuals are available in the College Bookstore and are on reserve in Ladd Library.

Modern Language Association of America. *MLA Handbook for Writers of Research Papers.*

Kate L. Turabian. *A Manual for Writers of Term Papers, Theses, and Dissertations* (University of Chicago Press).

University of Chicago Press. *A Manual of Style.*

C. Department Recommendations

Most departments at Bates College recommend either a particular guide or a major journal illustrating the form of citation most widely accepted in the field. A copy of each is on reserve in Ladd Library.

Anthropology: *American Anthropologist* (a major journal in the field)

Art: Sylvan Barnett, *A Short Guide to Writing About Art* (Boston: Little Brown)

Biology: Council of Biology Editors, *A Guide for Authors, Editors, and Publishers in the Biological Sciences*

Chemistry: Janet S. Dodd, *The American Chemical Society Style Guide: A Manual for Authors and Editors*

Economics: Use the author-date method as described in 1) K.L. Turabian, *A Manual for Writers of Term Papers, Theses, and Dissertations* (University of Chicago Press), or in 2) the Economics Department's handout "Preparing Papers and Theses: A Guide for Economics Students"

Education: K.L. Turabian, *A Manual for Writers of Term Papers, Theses, and Dissertations* (University of Chicago Press)

English: *MLA Handbook for Writers of Research Papers*

Foreign Languages: *MLA Handbook for Writers of Research Papers*

Geology: Geological Society of America: 1) Information for Contributors and 2) *Geological Society of America Bulletin*

History: K.L. Turabian, *A Manual for Writers of Term Papers, Theses, and Dissertations* (University of Chicago Press)

Mathematics: American Mathematical Society, *Manual for Authors*

Music: K.L. Turabian, *A Manual for Writers of Term Papers, Theses, and Dissertations* (University of Chicago Press)

Philosophy & Religion: 1) *MLA Handbook for Writers of Research Papers* and 2) author-date method

Physics & Astronomy: American Institute of Physics, *Style Manual*, prepared by David Hathwell and A.W. Kenneth Metzner

Political Science: K.L. Turabian, *A Manual for Writers of Term Papers, Theses, and Dissertations* (University of Chicago Press)

Psychology: American Psychological Association, *Publication Manual*

Sociology: *American Sociological Review* (a major journal) Theater & Rhetoric: *MLA Handbook for Writers of Research Papers*

Part IV: Two Common Methods of Citation

There are two widely used general methods of citation; most other forms are variations on these. In most of the humanities and social sciences, footnotes are used to cite works consulted. In most of the sciences, footnotes are avoided, and the author-date method of citation is used instead. Both of these methods are explained below; they should never be combined.

A. Modified Chicago Style
A1. General
The following paragraphs describe a system of scholarly citation commonly used in the humanities and most of the social sciences. It is based largely on the University of Chicago style followed by Turabian and by the *Manual of Style* of the University of Chicago Press. It differs in some particulars from the MLA style.

This chapter summarizes the expectations of many scholars in disparate fields of study; there are points on which not all of those who use this general format do as is indicated here.

For details not covered below, consult one of the style manuals listed in Part III above.

A2. Footnotes in General
A footnote is indicated in your text by a numerical superscript, i.e., a number in a raised position. This number should follow any punctuation except a dash. When you are acknowledging the source of a quotation, the footnote number should follow the end of the quoted matter. Footnote numbers in term papers should be consecutive throughout. Although many writers collect the footnotes at the end of the paper - between the text and bibliography - Turabian recommends typing the footnotes at the foot of each page. She also recommends typing or drawing a straight line of two inches, beginning at the left-hand margin, to make it clear to the reader where the text ends and the footnotes begin.

After this line, leave one line of typing blank, then begin the first footnote on the second line of typing. Introduce each footnote by a superior number (a superscript), on the same page where that number is used in the text. Single-space within each footnote, but double-space between successive footnotes on the same page.

A3. Footnotes: First Reference (Books)

The first reference to any published work should give complete bibliographical data on that work. This consists of the author's name, the complete title, the facts of publication, and an exact reference when appropriate. A page reference, for example, would ordinarily be appropriate for citing quotations.

For books, give the full names of all authors, in nominal order (i.e., first name or initial first), as in the following examples:

[1]Clarence Perkins, Clarence H. Matterson, and Reginald I. Lovell, *Modern Europe* (New York: Prentice-Hall, 1941), p. 802.

[2]T.S. Eliot, *Notes Towards a Definition of Culture* (New York: Harcourt, Brace, 1949), p. 106.

[3]J. William Fulbright, *The Arrogance of Power* (New York: Random House, 1966), pp.4-9.

If the person responsible for the book is an editor or compiler rather than an author in the strict sense, insert the appropriate abbreviation (for example, ed., eds., comp., comps.) following his or her name. Book titles should be underlined, and every word should be capitalized except for articles, conjunctions, and prepositions, but always capitalize the first word of a title or subtitle. If an edition other than the first is used, this should be specified in the following form:

[4]Leonard Bloom and Philip Selznick, *Sociology: A Text with Adapted Readings*, 4th ed. (New York: Harper & Row, 1968), pp. 126-127.

[5]Max Farrand, ed., *The Records of the Federal Convention of 1787*, rev. ed. (New Haven: Yale University Press, 1937), 1:64-65.

The facts of publication are enclosed in parentheses. The city of publication is given first, followed by a colon. "London" or "Philadelphia" is sufficient, but for unfamiliar places, also give the country (spelled out) or state (abbreviated) in which it is located (e.g., Englewood Cliffs, N.J.); give the country or state whenever ambiguity might otherwise arise (e.g., Cambridge, Mass.; London, Ont.). Spell the place name in English (e.g., Vienna, not Wien). The publisher's name follows, with "The," "Inc.," and "Ltd." omitted, "and Sons" usually omitted, "Company" abbreviated to "Co." or else omitted, "Brothers" abbreviated to "Bros." or else omitted, and the ampersand (&) substituted for the word *and*. The date of publication follows; publication over several years is indicated as, e.g., 1917-1921.

An exact reference to a chapter, page, or section may follow as in examples above. When you are citing a well-known text, of which there are several editions, and that text has fairly specific divisions other than pages, use the other divisions - e.g., sections within chapters, chapters within books, chapter and verse from books of the Bible, Stephanos numbers in Plato, Bekker numbers in Aristotle, lines or stanzas of long poems, and act, scene, and line in Shakespeare's plays. These are most likely to be standard from edition to edition, whereas page numbers vary.

Here are some examples:

Exodus 20:15.

Plato, *Meno* 82a-85d.

Cicero, *Laws* 3. 1. 2-3. [This means book 3, chapter 1, sections 2-3. It could also be cited as "III.i. 2-3," or, least ambiguously, as "bk. 3, ch. 1, secs. 2-3." If your specific citation begins with a word or abbreviation rather than a number, it should be preceded by a comma, as in the following example.]

T.S. Eliot, *The Waste Land*, lines 67-77. [In contexts where omission of the author's name would cause no confusion, it is often considered permis- sible to omit it in cases such as this one; compare the next example.]

Romeo and Juliet 3. 1. 94-95. [This could also be cited as "III. i. 94-95" or as "act 3, sc. 1, lines 94-95"; the latter would be preceded by a comma. Shakespeare's name need not be given.]

In some contexts and for some audiences it is appropriate to abbreviate author's names and titles of works such as the above, especially those of biblical texts and classical Greek and Roman materials. Turabian recommends that the writer consult the *Oxford Classical Dictionary* for a list of accepted abbreviations of classical names.

A4. Footnotes: First Reference (Journal Articles)
The title of a journal article should be enclosed in quotation marks and not underlined. Capitalize it as you would a book title, and follow it with a comma. The name of the journal follows, capitalized as with a book title, and underlined. Here are examples of journal article citations in the modified Chicago style:

[6]Brian Barry, "John Rawls and the Priority of Liberty," *Philosophy and Public Affairs*, 2 (1973): 283.

[7]Robert A. Gordon, "Issues in Multiple Regression," *American Journal of Sociology*, 73 (1968): 595-596.

[8]J. G. A. Pocock, "Machiavelli, Harrington, and English Political Ideologies in the Eighteenth Century," *William and Mary Quarterly*, ser. 3, 22 (1965): 549-550.

A volume and page reference normally follows, in the form "15 (1970): 405-413," meaning, volume 15, pages 405 through 413, which was published in the year 1970. Note that this style uses Arabic numerals for volume numbers; certain other styles use Roman numerals instead, in the form "XV (1970), 405-413."

Also note that in the last of the sample footnotes above, a series designation precedes the volume number. Although Turabian prefers citing page numbers without giving all of the second of two inclusive numbers (e.g., 405-13 rather than 405-413), the use of complete page numbers takes little time or space, and reduces the chances of error.

Some writers give the "number" or "part" of a journal when citing an article from it. This is particularly helpful to readers when the article cited is in a recent volume, and would not yet be bound. You can cite the "number" in various ways, some of which are illustrated below:

> [8]Sheldon S. Wolin, "The Politics of Self-Disclosure," *Political Theory*, vol. 4, no. 3 (August 1976), p. 325.

> [10]Sheldon S. Wolin, "The Politics of Self-Disclosure," *Political Theory*, 4, no. 3 (August 1976): 325.

> [11]Sheldon S. Wolin, "The Politics of Self-Disclosure," *Political Theory*, vol. IV, no. 3 (August 1976), p. 325.

> [12]Sheldon S. Wolin, "The Politics of Self-Disclosure," *Political Theory*, IV,3 (August 1976): 325.

Note that "vol." and "p." (or "pp.") are either both used or both omitted.

Many cases that are not treated here, such as the citation of poetry, and court opinions, are covered by Turabian and other stylebooks.

A5. Footnotes: Subsequent References
Once a work has been cited in full, subsequent references to that same work may be indicated in an abbreviated form as in the following examples:

> [13]Perkins et al., pp. 700-701.
> [14]Farrand, ed., 1:66.
> [15]Wolin, p. 326.
> [16]Ibid., p. 325.

Note that each of these has been cited before, and that the titles of the works have been omitted. The omission of the title is permissible only if no ambiguity would arise, but if you cite from more than one work by the same author - and must therefore indicate which of these works you are citing in a subsequent reference - you may shorten the titles as a matter of convenience. If, for example, in addition to having cited Brian Barry's article "John Rawls and the Priority of Liberty" (n.6, above), you had cited his book *The Liberal Theory of Justice*, you could make reference to both of these previously cited works in the following, abbreviated form:

> [17]Barry, "John Rawls," p.284.
> [18]Farrand, ed., 1:66.
> [19]Barry, *Liberal Theory*, pp. 1-5.

The abbreviation "ibid." (for *ibidem*, in the same place) stands for everything in the previous footnote except for whatever follows the "ibid." By itself (i.e., without a page or other reference number), "ibid." designates the very same place as the footnote immediately preceding it, as specified by the page or other reference number contained in it.

A6. Bibliographical Entries: Order of Data
In this system of citation, the order of bibliographical data about books is as follows: author, title, place of publication, publisher, and date. For an article, it is as follows: author, title, name of journal, volume number, date, and inclusive page numbers of the entire article.

A7. Bibliographical Entries: Author
All works should be alphabetized by the last name of the author. In this system of citation, works by the same author (or group of coauthors) are arranged alphabetically by title or chronologically. Authors are listed with their last names first. Some writers list all authors this way; but for works with more than one author, many writers list the second and subsequent authors' first names first.

A8. Bibliographical Entries: Titles, Editions, and Volumes of Books
After the author's name comes the title, which should be underlined. It should be given exactly as it appears on the title page, including the subtitle, if any. Titles in non-Latin alphabets should be transliterated. Capitalize every word in the title, except for articles, conjunctions, and prepositions; always capitalize the first word of a title or subtitle.

If an edition other than the first is used, this is indicated after the title. The number of volumes, if more than one, is indicated after the title or edition number, as in the following examples:

> Bloom, Leonard, and Philip Selznick. *Sociology: A Text with Adapted Readings.* 4th ed. New York: Harper & Row, 1968.

> Malone, Dumas. *Jefferson and His Time.* 6 vols. Boston: Little, Brown, 1948-75.

> Popper, Karl R. *The Open Society and Its Enemies.* 5th ed., rev. 2 vols. Princeton: Princeton University Press, 1966.

A9. Bibliographical Entries: Publication Data for Books
The publication data for books consists of the place of publication, followed by a colon; then the publisher, followed by a comma; then the year of publication, terminated by a period. None of this is enclosed in parentheses, but in other respects it conforms to the guidelines given for footnotes in Section A3, above.

A10. Bibliographical Entries: Journal Article Data
Bibliographical references to journal articles follow the same format as those for footnote references, except that the author's name is given last name first and followed by a period (as with books), and that the inclusive page numbers of the entire article are given.

A11. Bibliographical Entries: Contributed Chapters, Symposia, Short Literary Works
If one author has written a chapter or contributed an article to a book or symposium volume of which someone else is the editor or principal author, list the chapter or article and cite the whole collection as well:

Chatman, Seymour, ed. and trans. *Literary Style: A Symposium.* London and New York: Oxford University Press, 1969.

Wellek, Rene. "Stylistics, Poetics, and Criticism," pp. 65-75 in *Literary Style: A Symposium*, ed. and trans. Seymour Chatman. London and New York: Oxford University Press, 1969.

Similarly, include in your bibliography a poem, short story, essay, or other literary work which appeared in an anthology or collection, and cite the collection as well:

Matthias, John, ed. *23 Modern British Poets.* Chicago: Swallow Press, 1971. [Note: this anthology should be alphabetized as if its title were spelled out, "Twenty-three...."]

Thomas, D.M. "Elegy for an Android," p. 192 in *23 Modern British Poets,* ed. John Matthias. Chicago: Swallow Press, 1971.

A12. Citation of Unavailable Works Through Secondary Citations

In the interests of thoroughness, or of providing useful information to your reader, you may often want to cite a work that you have been unable to obtain for your own use. You may cite the original work, provided you acknowledge that you are relying on a secondhand account, as in the following example:

[20]John Calvin, *Joannis Calvini Opera Selecta*, vol. 1, p. 139, quoted in T. H. L. Parker, *John Calvin: A Biography* (Philadelphia: Westminster Press, 1975), p. 44.

In your bibliography:

Calvin, John. *Joannis Calvini Opera Selecta*, ed. P. Barth, W. Niesel, and D. Scheuner, vol. 1. Munich: C. Kaiser, 1952. Quoted in Parker.

Parker, T. H. L. *John Calvin: A Biography.* Philadelphia: Westminster Press, 1975.

A13. Citation of Theses, Typescripts, and Manuscripts

Cite unpublished material in a footnote to your text giving the author's name, the title if there is one, the nature of the material, and, when pertinent, where the manuscript can be located. In the case of theses the appropriate designation - undergraduate thesis, honors thesis, master's thesis, or Ph.D. dissertation - should be given.

[21]Robert William Pladek, "Politics in the Funnies: The Influence of Political Cartoons on Public Perception of Political Leaders" (Honors thesis, Bates College, 1976), p. 10.

[22]Marilyn Lamond, "Eugene Scribe and the Spanish Theater, 1834-1850" (Ph.D. dissertation, University of North Carolina, 1958), p. 137.

[23]Thomas Mann to Mrs. Edward M. Powell, 2 December 1940. William Lyon Phelps Collection Letters, Bates College Library, Lewiston, Maine.

In your bibliography:

Lamond, Marilyn. "Eugene Scribe and the Spanish Theater, 1834-1850." Ph.D. dissertation, University of North Carolina, 1958.

Mann, Thomas. Letter to Mrs. Edward M. Powell, 2 December 1940. (Typescript, William Lyon Phelps Collection Letters, Bates College Li- brary, Lewiston, Maine).

Pladek, Robert William. "Politics in the Funnies: The Influence of Political Cartoons on Public Perception of Political Leaders." Honors thesis, Bates College, 1976.

A14. Citation of Other Materials

Motion pictures and sound recordings, if copyrighted, may be handled as published material, with a lower case *c* inserted before the year, e.g., c1971. For a motion picture, indicate the size (in mm) and add the word *sound* if there is a sound track:

U.S. National Institute of Mental Health. *Drug Abuse.* 16mm motion picture, color, sound. Released by National Audiovisual Center, c1971.

For sound recordings, specify whether a disc, tape, or another form. Give the speed and additional information as in the following example:

Gould, Glenn. *Glenn Gould: Concert Dropout, in Conversation with John McClure.* Phonodisc, 33 1/3 rpm, stereophonic, 2 sides. Columbia Records BS 15, c1968.

Cite commercial computer software by stating name of program writer, title of program, descriptive label, distributor, year of publication, number of kilobytes, operating system, and form of program (disk, cassette, etc.):

Bradley, Drake R. *DATASIM.* Computer software. Bates College, 1987. IBM-PC, disk.

Unpublished speeches and interviews are listed in your bibliography under the name of the speaker or the person interviewed, followed by the title or a description and the date:

Carter, Jimmy. Bates College Democratic Caucus, Lewiston, Maine. Speech, December 11, 1975.

Lennon, John. NBC Television Network, New York. Interview, September 15, 1975.

Reynolds, T. Hedley. "An American Primer: A Panoramic View of American History Since 1776." Charles Grant Memorial Lecture, Middlebury College, March 29, 1976.

Works of art may be cited in footnote form, but if you cite many such works it is preferable to include a "List of Illustrations" or other comparable list at the end of your paper. References to this list are by Arabic numbers, standing without punctuation in the outside left margin of your text. The list itself usually gives the name of the artist, the birth and death dates, the title of the work, and the year of its completion. The form and medium of the work are then given, followed by the dimensions if the work is flat (painting or drawing as opposed to sculpture or architecture). The ownership is usually given last. These points are illustrated in the following examples:

CHURCH, FREDERIC EDWIN (1826-1900)
⁶*Niagara Falls*, 1857. Oil on canvas, 159 x 286 cm. Collection of the Corcoran Gallery of Art, Washington.

⁷*Iceberg*, 1891. Oil on canvas, 51 x 76 cm. Museum of Art, Carnegie Institute, Pittsburgh.

If you have not seen the original work, but only a reproduction in a book or article, you should also indicate the source you used, in the manner indicated by sections A3 through A5, above.

B. Author-Date Method

B1. General
In the sciences there is less agreement on bibliographical style than in the humanities, though the majority of natural scientists do follow the author-date format in some version.

The following format adheres closely to that of *A Guide for Authors, Editors, and Publishers in the Biological Sciences* (see Part III, above), and also the style recommended for scientific writing by Turabian (chapter 12, superseding most of chapters 6-8) and by the *Chicago Manual of Style*.

B2. Citations in Text
In the author-date method, *footnotes are not used* as a means of citing sources. Instead of presenting bibliographical data in a footnote, the author and date are given thus:

According to Smith (1960),...
Smith (1960) demonstrated that...
...was demonstrated (Smith, 1960).

Each of the above implies that the reader can find *in your bibliography* a full reference to a work published in 1960 by Smith, in which are contained whatever ideas or words you have cited. Note that the citation must precede a period or other terminal punctuation, as in the last example above.

B3. Variant Forms of Citation
A work with two or more authors is cited as "Smith and Jones (1960)" or as "Smith et al. (1960)." If more than one person named Smith is included in your bibliography, specify "J. Smith (1960)." If Smith published more than one paper in the same year list them as "Smith (1960a)" and "Smith (1960b)," both in your text and in the bibliography. If you have quoted Smith directly, indicate the exact page, in the form "Smith (1960, p. 18)" or "Smith (1960: 18)." Page references (and, similarly,

table or figure references) may be desirable in certain other instances as well. Page references to a multi-volume book may be in the form "Davis (1950, 2:125)" or else "Davis (1950, vol. 2, p. 125)." If the volumes are separately listed in the bibliography, they may be cited as, e.g., "Davis (1950b: 125)."

B4. Bibliographical Entries: Authors
All works are alphabetized by the last name of the author. In the author-date format, works by the same author are arranged in chronological order of their publication. Within each entry, the order is as follows: author, date, title, publication data.

If there are several authors, the names of all except the first should be in nominal order (first name first). If a work is authored by a corporate body, list the work under the name of the corporate body as author (e.g., United States Public Health Service). If the person responsible for a work is an editor, cite as "(ed.)" or "(eds.)" following the name.

B5. Bibliographical Entries: Dates of Publication
Write out the year in full, e.g., 1896, not '96. If publication continues over several years, cite as 1912-1913, for example, not 1912-13. If several works by the same author (or the same set of coauthors) are published in the same year, list them as 1954a, 1954b, and 1954c, for example.

Because the date cited is that of publication, no date can be cited here for any type of unpublished material without giving the mistaken impression that the work has in fact been published. The date (if any) is cited in a different manner, described in Section B11, below.

B6. Bibliographical Entries: Titles
Reproduce the title in full, exactly as it appears on the title page of the work. Subtitles may be omitted if desired. Non-Latin alphabets should be transliterated. Use "sentence capitalization," i.e., capitalize only the first word of the title, any proper names, and other words that you would normally capitalize in ordinary text. Some persons prefer "title capitalization" for books (capitalizing all words except articles, conjunctions, and prepositions), and "sentence capitalization" for journal articles. (In German titles, capitalize every noun.)

In the author-date format, titles are neither underlined nor enclosed in quotation marks.

B7. Bibliographical Entries: Publication Data on Books
The place of publication follows the title, spelled out in English (e.g., Vienna, not Wien). Add the name of the country or state if the city is unfamiliar (e.g., Garden City, N.Y.) or if ambiguity might otherwise arise (e.g., Cambridge, Mass.; London, Ont.; Portland, Ore.). Following this data, give the name of the publisher, omitting "Brothers," "Sons," and "Inc.," and either abbreviating "Company" as "Co." or leaving it out altogether. After giving the publisher's name, you may give the total number of pages, e.g., 233 pp.

Editions other than the first should be identified as such, following the title. Multi-volume works may be cited as a single work by adding, e.g., 3 vols., instead of the number of pages; you may instead list each volume separately, citing, e.g., vol. 2, with or without inclusive page numbers of the volume, at the end of the bibliographical entry. Here are some examples:

> Bolk, Louis, Ernst Goppert, Erich Kallius, and Wilhelm Lubosch. 1931- 1939.
> Handbuch der vergleichenden Anatomie der Wirbeltiere. Berlin and Vienna,

Urban and Schwarzenberg, 6 vols. [Note that this would be cited in your text as Bolk et al. (1931-1939).]

Hall, E. Raymond, and Keith R. Kelson. 1959. The mammals of North America. New York, Ronald Press, 2 vols.

Kormondy, Edward J. 1969. Concepts of ecology. Englewood Cliffs, N.J., Prentice-Hall, 209 pp.

Lindsay, Robert Bruce. 1969. The nature of physics, a physicist's view on the history and philosophy of his science. Providence, R.I., Brown University Press, 212 pp. [Subtitle and pages optional.]

Raup, David M., and Steven M. Stanley. 1971. Principles of paleontology. San Francisco, W. H. Freeman, 388 pp.

Stebbins, G. Ledyard. 1971. Processes of organic evolution. 2nd ed. Englewood Cliffs, N.J., Prentice-Hall.

Washburn, Sherwood L. (ed.) 1963. Classification and human evolution. Chicago, Aldine. 371 pp.

International Commission on Zoological Nomenclature. 1964. Code international de nomenclature zoologique adopté par le XVe congrès international de zoologie. International code of zoological nomenclature adopted by the XV international congress of zoology. London, International Trust for Zoological Nomenclature. [This work, with corporate author, has a "split" title page, with both French and English title given.]

Anonymous. 1956. General guide to the American Museum of Natural History. New York, Man and Nature Publications, American Museum of Natural History. [Practice varies on the citation of anonymous works. [Listing under "Anonymous" as the author seems awkward to some people, but it does permit citing the work in the text as Anonymous (1956)]. Alternatives include listing the work by its title, with the date at the end, or where possible under a corporate author-here, the American Museum of Natural History.]

B8. Bibliographical Entries: Contributed Chapters and Symposia

If one author has written a chapter or contributed an article to a book or symposium volume of which someone else is the editor or principal author, list that chapter or article as in the following examples:

Huber, Ernst. 1933. The facial musculature and its innervation. *In* Hartman, Carl G., and William L. Straus, Jr. (eds.), 1933. The Anatomy of the Rhesus Monkey, New York, Hafner Publishing Co., chapter 8, pp. 176- 188.

Hartman, Carl G., and William L. Straus, Jr. (eds.). 1933. The Anatomy of the Rhesus Monkey *(Macaca mulatta)*. New York, Hafner Publishing Co., ix+383 pp.

In the entry for the included chapter by Huber, note that the chapter title uses "sentence capitalization" even when the title of the larger work uses "title capitalization." Note that the name of the larger work is introduced by *In*, both capitalized and underlined, that the (optional) subtitle has been omitted, and that the page numbers refer to Huber's chapter only. Note also that the larger work by Hartman and Straus is separately cited with its full title (including the optional subtitle), and that the page numbers cited are those of the entire book. *Macaca mulatta* is italicized only because it is the scientific name of a species and would therefore be italicized even in an ordinary sentence. Here is another example, taken from a collection by Washburn cited in section B7, above:

> Goodman, Morris. 1963. Man's place in the phylogeny of the primates as reflected in serum proteins. *In* Sherwood L. Washburn (ed.), Classification and human evolution (Chicago, Aldine), pp. 204-234.

If the editor of a collection contributes a paper or chapter of his or her own, which you use, list both the entire work and the contributed article. For example, to cite the article which Washburn himself wrote for the above-cited collection, change the reference given in B7 to read "Washburn, Sherwood L. (ed.) 1963a..." and cite the included article as follows:

> Washburn, Sherwood L. 1963b. Behavior and human evolution. *In* Sherwood L. Washburn (ed.), Classification and human evolution (Chicago, Aldine), pp. 190-203.

B9. Bibliographic Entries: Journal Articles Following the title of the article, give the name of the journal in which it appears. In bibliographical entries, avoid underlining, italics, and quotation marks. Keep abbreviations to a minimum. Never abbreviate the names of cities (e.g., London, not Lond.) or single-word titles like Ecology. As a rule, words ending in "-ology" are abbreviated as "-ol.," e.g., embryol., bacteriol., sociol.; but use "anthrop." rather than "anthropol." The following are considered standard, permissible, abbreviations:

Amer.	American
Bull.	Bulletin
Hist.	History or Historical
J. or Jour.	Journal
Proc.	Proceedings
Rev.	Review
Sci.	Science or Scientific
Soc.	Society, Société, etc.

The volume *(tome, Band)* number is given, followed by a colon; this number may be underlined. The inclusive page numbers are then given, as, e.g., 413-414 (never as 413-14 or 413-4). The particular issue of the journal (number, fascicule, part, *Heft*) may be cited within parentheses, e.g., 14 (2): 23-29, meaning, vol. 14, number 2, pages 23-29. Here are some examples of journal article bibliographical entries in the author-date format:

> Haines, R. Wheeler. 1939. A revision of the extensor muscles of the forearm in tetrapods. J. Anatomy, 73 (2): 211-233. [Note that "Anatomy," usually abbreviated "Anat.," has been spelled out to avoid any possible confusion with the French *Journal d'Anatomie*.]

_____. 1958. Arboreal or terrestrial ancestry of placental mammals. Quart. Rev. Biol., 33 (1): 1-23. [Note that when a series of works by one author is listed, the author's name is not spelled out in the second and subsequent entries, but is replaced by an underline of seven or ten typed spaces.]

When a journal is divided into series, the series designation is presented in parentheses before the volume number; this designation may be a number, a letter, or the abbreviation *n.s.* (for "new series"), as in the following examples:

Hill, J. P. 1932. The developmental history of the primates. Philos. Trans. Royal. Soc. London (B) 211: 45-178.

Green, Eunice Chace. 1935. Anatomy of the rat. Trans. Amer. Philos. Soc. (n.s.) 27: 1-370.

B10. Citation of Unavailable Works Through Secondary Citation

In the interests of thoroughness, or of providing useful information to your reader, you may often want to cite a work that you have been unable to obtain for your own use. You may cite the original work, provided you acknowledge that you are relying on a secondhand account, as in the following example:

(In your text:)
In another study, Bartrum (1941, cited by Pettijohn, 1957) concluded that...

(In your bibliography:)
Bartrum, J.A. 1941. Cone-in-cone and other structures in New Zealand coals. New Zealand J. Sci.Technol., (B) 22: 209-215. [Cited by Pettijohn, 1957.]

Pettijohn, F.J. 1957. Sedimentary rocks, 2nd ed. New York, Harper & Row.

B11. Citation of Theses, Typescripts, and Manuscripts

Cite unpublished writing in your text as, e.g., Jones (MS), and list them in your bibliography as, e.g., Jones, John P. MS. It is most important that a date not be included here - where it would be mistaken for a date of publication - because the work is unpublished. Following the title, insert data such as the following: Undergraduate thesis, Bates College, April, 1967. Senior theses, master's theses, and Ph.D. theses can all be handled in this way. For other types of manuscripts, information should be given that would tell the reader where to go to find the original, e.g., Unpublished manuscript, available at Houghton Library, Harvard University.

Here are some examples:

Stratton, Charles William IV. MS. The reduction of triple bonds in a solution containing titanium III. Honors thesis, Bates College, 1967.

Smith, Eloise Lane. MS. General outline of the pageant of Bates College. Typescript, 1939, on deposit in Bates College Library.

Poets make good doctors, or a guide to careers in the health field for Bates students. Mimeographed pamphlet, Bates College, no date.

Chute, Robert M. MS. Breakage and re-union of DNA fragments and a plasmid using restriction enzyme R.EcoR1 and ligase. Dittoed, 1 p.

Einstein, Albert. MS. [Letter to F.D. Roosevelt, August 2, 1939.] (Note that the description of an untitled work is enclosed in square brackets.)

B12. Citation of Other Materials

Motion pictures and sound recordings, if copyrighted, may be handled as published material, with a lower case *c* inserted before the year, e.g., c1965. For a motion picture indicate the size (in mm), and add the word *sound* if there is a sound track.

Washburn, Sherwood L. Irven Devore. c1962. Baboon Behavior. 16mm motion picture, color, sound. Available from University of California Extension Media Center, Berkeley, California 94720. [The information concerning availability might be helpful to your reader.]

For sound recordings, specify whether a disc, a tape, or another form. Give the speed and additional information as in the following example:

A field guide to bird songs of eastern and central North America. Phonodisc, 33 1/3 rpm, 4 sides. Boston, Houghton Mifflin Co., c1959. [An anonymous work; may be listed by title or under "Anonymous."]

Cite commercial computer software by stating name of program writer, date, title of program, descriptive label, distributor, number of kilobytes, operating system, and form of program (disk, cassette, etc.):

Bradley, Drake R. 1987. DATASIM. Computer software. Bates College. IBM-PC, disk.

Unpublished speeches are listed in your bibliography under the speaker's name, followed by the title or description and the date. If there is no title, the description is enclosed in square brackets:

Carter, Jimmy. [Address to Bates College Democratic Caucus, Lewiston, Maine, Dec. 11, 1975.]

Personal communications of any form addressed to you are not ordinarily listed in the bibliography, but should be cited in the text as, e.g., Jones (personal communication). Correspondence not directed to you personally is treated as a manuscript (see B11, Einstein example).

Part V: Judicial Procedures

Students are held responsible for reading this document. The College assumes that failure to observe the principles summarized in Parts I and II is not accidental. As the Faculty Statement of Policy on Plagiarism says, the absence of any discernible attempt to give credit to your source will be taken as *prima facie* evidence of an intent to plagiarize. In other words, if you have made no attempt to give credit to someone else, you have created a presumption of willful plagiarism.

If academic dishonesty of any kind is suspected, redress is sought through judicial procedures outlined in the *Student Handbook*. First, the Dean of Students is notified by the person making the accusation. After discussions with the Dean, full judicial redress may be sought through the Committee on Student Conduct.

What is plagiarism?

We've gathered together a number of resources to help faculty and students alike get their bearings on the subject in general and this resource site in particular.

Introduction

We've produced a basic <u>primer</u> on academic honesty and plagiarism. This is a good place to begin to understand what exactly is meant by plagiarism and what kinds of practices, intentional or inadvertent, constitute it.

Bibliography

We've compiled a <u>bibliography</u> of print and electronic resources dedicated to plagiarism.

Style Guides

We've assembled a list of the various <u>style guides</u> regularly used in the academy and have provided links to online versions where available.

Tutorials and Guides

We have produced several resources to help students test their understanding of plagiarism, familiarize themselves with citations, and to learn the basics about Endnote, a bibliographical software program:

Self-Test: An online quiz that tests your knowledge of what does and does not constitute plagiarism.

Citation Examples: Dynamic examples of correct and incorrect citation and paraphrasing.

Endnote: A basic introduction to the bibliographic management program.

Academic Honesty

A quick look at this site's <u>weblog</u> establishes that colleges and universities take the issue of plagiarism extremely seriously. Students at all levels should acquaint themselves with the various practices that constitute plagiarism, including:

- Submission of academic work that is not the student's own original effort;
- Use of the same work for multiple courses without prior consent of the instructors;
- Unacknowledged references to sources beyond those authorized by the instructor in preparing papers, constructing reports, solving problems, or carrying out other academic assignments;
- Inadequate, incorrect, or mistaken citation of any source.

Most people do not deliberately commit plagiarism. Usually, it results from:

Procrastination: It is important to set aside adequate time to complete your assignment. When using sources, you should get in the habit of citing them in full as you write. Filling in page numbers, making footnotes, or making a works cited page or bibliography after you have finished writing often leads to inadvertent mis-citations or omissions.

Incomplete understanding of original material: Avoid using any source with which you are not completely comfortable. As a general rule, if you cannot restate the main idea of a passage in your own words without referring to the original source, then you should not use this source for your own work.

Citation Errors: Common errors that lead to accidental plagiarism include: using words or passages from the original source without using quotation marks and/or without citing the source; using different citation formats within the same assignment; or using a citation format incorrectly.

Poor note-taking: Inexperienced students often forget to put quotation marks around notes taken directly from text, or find that their notes are disorganized. As a result, they cannot tell which notes came from which source when they are in the stages of writing up their assignment.

Professors assign papers/projects to determine your own analysis and ideas on a topic; they already know what the established sources have to say and are instead looking for fresh perspectives. If you are able to take academic risks by introducing new and insightful ideas about a topic, you are far less likely to commit accidental plagiarism because the foundation of your work will be your own. Learning to develop your own insight on a topic is, after all, one goal of a college education.

Understanding the Complexities of Plagiarism

It is important to understand that plagiarism is not always a cut and dry issue. It is not only committed by students, and when it occurs it is often defended on the basis that it was not intended (see the weblog's recent entries for discussion of the case of <u>Doris Kearns Goodwin</u>). Inadvertent plagiarism is nevertheless plagiarism. Familiarizing yourself with the following concepts and practices should help you come to terms with what is plagiarism so that you can avoid it:

1. <u>Overview of Plagiarism: Common Types of Plagiarism</u>
2. <u>Common Knowledge</u>
3. <u>Note taking</u>
4. <u>Citing Sources</u>

Overview of Terms: The Common Types of Plagiarism

"To plagiarize" comes from the Latin word "<u>plagiare</u>" which means, "to kidnap." There are many ways to "kidnap" or steal ideas, both intentional and unintentional. As a member of an academic community that takes the sharing of ideas and information very seriously, it is important to avoid even the suspicion of plagiarism. To that end, it is your responsibility to learn how to cite your sources. It is also important to remember that understanding your materials is paramount to writing a good paper, and that plagiarizing reveals a lack of confidence in your own understanding. If you are ever tempted to kidnap someone else's words or ideas – think again – and go to your professor for help.

There are different types and degrees of plagiarism. We've defined the most common types below and have provided links to examples.

Direct Plagiarism

Direct plagiarism is the word-for-word transcription of a section of someone else's work without attribution. The deliberate plagiarism of someone else's work is unethical, academically dishonest, and grounds for disciplinary actions, including expulsion. [<u>See example</u>.]

Self Plagiarism

Self-plagiarism occurs when a student submits his or her own previous work, or mixes parts of previous works, without permission from **all** professors involved. For example, it would be unacceptable to incorporate part of a term paper you wrote in high school into a paper assigned in a college course. Self-plagiarism also applies to submitting the same

piece of work for assignments in different classes without previous permission from **both** professors.

Mosaic Plagiarism

Mosaic Plagiarism occurs when a student borrows phrases from a source without using quotation marks, or finds synonyms for the author's language while keeping to the same general structure and meaning of the original. Sometimes called "patch writing," this kind of paraphrasing, **whether intentional or not**, is academically dishonest and punishable – even if you footnote your source! [See example.]

Accidental Plagiarism

Accidental plagiarism occurs when a person neglects to cite their sources, or misquotes their sources, or unintentionally paraphrases a source by using similar words, groups of words, and/or sentence structure without attribution. (See example for mosaic plagiarism.) Students should learn how to cite their sources and to take careful and accurate notes when doing research. (See the Note-Taking section on the Academic Honesty page.) Cases of accidental plagiarism are taken seriously and they can be brought before a school's judiciary board.

Common Knowledge

A statement considered to be "common knowledge" does not need to be attributed to a source. Facts that can be found in numerous places and are likely to be found by many people are likewise considered common knowledge. For example, it is common knowledge that Nathaniel Hawthorne and Franklin Pierce were famous graduates of Bowdoin College. However, it is **not** common knowledge that President Pierce appointed Hawthorne as the U.S. Consul in Liverpool in appreciation of the author's campaign biography of candidate Pierce in 1852. This latter fact is proposed by Charles Calhoun, A Small College in Maine: Two Hundred Years of Bowdoin (Brunswick: Bowdoin College, 1993), pp. 164-165.

As a general rule well-known or basic facts do not need to be documented; however, interpretations of such facts do.

If something is not common knowledge, or if you are not certain whether it is or not, cite the source. During the course of your studies, you will need to be able to distinguish between different kinds of common knowledge: common knowledge for the general public versus common knowledge for a specialized audience.

Plagiarism Information

As stated in the **CSB/SJU Plagiarism Policy**, plagiarism can result from either deliberate dishonesty or ignorance of citation procedures. This page is intended to give **College of St. Benedict/St. John's University** faculty and students some guidance in dealing with both situations.

Contents:

-
-
-
-
-
-

Teaching for Academic Integrity

There are numerous pedagogical strategies to discourage plagiarism in student writing. Some excellent practical ideas are suggested in the following readings, some of which also make good springboards to discussion with students.

What is the Price of Plagiarism?
Karoun Demirjian, *The Christian Science Monitor*.

Creating Plagiarism-Proof Assignments
Barbara Fister, Gustavus Adolphus College

How Teachers Can Reduce Cheating's Lure
Mark Clayton, *The Christian Science Monitor*, Monday October 27, 1997.

Plagiarism
Princeton University Writing Center, 1999. Clear definitions and examples to use in the classroom. Also consider using **Plagiarism: What It is and How to Recognize and Avoid It** Writing Tutorial Services, Indiana University.

Plagiarism and Anti-Plagiarism
Heyward Ehrlich, Department of English, Rutgers University.

Plagiarism PowerPoint Presentation
Created by David Arnott for the College of Saint Benedict/Saint John's University, this is a PowerPoint presentation and a teacher's guide for faculty.

Downloadable Term Papers: What's a Prof to Do?
Tom Rocklin , Department of Psychology, University of Iowa.

Anti-Plagiarism Strategies for Research Papers
Robert Harris, Vanguard University of Southern California.

The Death and Rebirth of Plagiarism
Rodney P. Riegle, Department of Education, Illinois State University.

Citing Sources
Plagiarism can occur when a student is ignorant of correct citational procedures. Students and faculty can consult our page for help with "generally-accepted" methods of citing electronic as well as print materials.

Plagiarism Tutorials

A number of universities have designed tutorials to help students understand the nature and implications of plagiarism:

Joining the Scholarly Conversation: Scholarly Research and Academic Integrity (Georgetown University)

Bedford/St. Martin's Plagiarism Workshop (http://bcs.bedfordstmartins.com/plagiarism/)

Plagiarism: What it is and how to avoid it (Montgomery College, ML)
(http://www.montgomerycollege.edu/library/plagiarismintro.htm)

Plagiarism Court: You Be the Judge. (Fairfield University, CT)
(library2.fairfield.edu/instruction/ramona/plugin.html)

Looking for a Plagiarized Full-Text Document

Begin with the student's bibliography and search our most heavily used full-text databases: EBSCOHost and **LexisNexis Academic**, both of which are comprised of several different databases.

EBSCOHost databases, including **Academic Search Premier**, the **Business Source Premier**, **Regional Business News**, **MasterFILE Premier**, and **Catholic Periodical and Literature Index** provide hundreds of thousands of full-text articles. These databases are very user-friendly and popular with students.
To search for words in the text select the "Full Text" limit option, and look for unique words or phrases from the suspect text.

LexisNexis Academic
Go to "Guided News Search," select "full text" and type in the phrase you are seeking. Adjacent words (for example, cellular phone, automobile accident, etc.) are searched for as a phrase. The most popular resources used are the 50+ major newspapers (some of which are foreign) in the "Top News" and "General News" topics, but full text can also be found in the following sections:

- Company News

- Industry & Market News

- Government & Political News

- Legal News

- Law Reviews

- Biographical Information

- Reference & Directories

Other library full-text databases currently include **JSTOR**, **Project Muse**, **ProQuest Religion Databases**, and **Science Direct**

JSTOR
In **Basic Search** mode, type in your phrase, without quotes, making sure that the drop-down menu says "full-text". In **Advanced Search** mode, you must put quotation marks (" ") around your phrase.

Project MUSE
To search a phrase in Project Muse journals, you must use single quotes (' ').

Consider searching in other **subscription databases in the appropriate subject area,** Use the ⟳Find It button to see if the libraries have full text access to a particular article.

Try searching a suspicious text string in **Google Scholar** or **Google Book**

Looking for a Plagiarized Web Page

You may try phrase searching for a certain unique phrase in your favorite search engine.

- <u>Google</u> - put the phrase in quotes (" ")

- <u>Alta Vista</u> - put the phrase in quotes (" ")

- <u>HotBot</u> - choose "exact phrase" on its drop-down menu

- <u>Yahoo</u> - put the phrase in quotes (" ")

- <u>WebCrawler</u> - put the phrase in quotes (" ")

Finding the Phrase on the Page If the phrase you are seeking appears in the web pages your search retrieves, it may be highlighted and easily found. If it is not, use the "find" function on the browser (click on "Edit" on the top line, then on "Find in Page") to go the exact point where the phrase appears.

Plagiarism From a Book
You may need check the items listed in the Works Cited list and visit the stacks. If the majority or most important sources the essay cites are **not** in MnPALS or at CSB/SJU, check to see what the student knows about Interlibrary Loan services.

Look for a **MnPALS** <electronic resource> option after the title. Click it open to view the title online, and use the "search this eBook" box to look for a suspicious text string. CSB/SJU currently have access to approximately 7000 eBooks.

Amazon.com may allow you to "search inside this book." Type your text string into the search box, using quotations. If that exact phrase occurs in any of Amazon.com's 33+ million pages of searchable text, you will be be able to view that text online. Read an Amazon.com **press release about Search Inside.**

Term Paper Web Sites
The Paper Store
> Also has an 800 number to order pre- or custom-written papers. Has a *big* disclaimer about academic honesty, and claims to exist only for educational purposes.

Cheathouse.com
> For $9.95 a year you get access to the database of 9500 essays, complete with the original author's age and type of institution, the original grade and teacher's comments.

Research Papers Online
> Guarantees lowest prices, all-new papers never before circulated. Prices seem to run about $10.00 per page.

The Essay Depot
> Claims to have thousands of pre-written papers contributed by students, available for free download.

Term Papers on File
> $9.95 s per page for pre-written papers; custom research for $19.95 per page. Warns users that "No Document May Be Reprinted Without Proper Attribution To Our Company As The Original Source".

Electronic Term Papers

Examples of a wide array of privately posted student research collections:

CSB/SJU Libraries Annual Research Bibliography Awards
Previous winners have made excellent use of Alcuin and Clemens Libraries resources and services.

The Rutgers Scholar
an electronic bulletin of undergraduate research from Rutgers University

Student Research Papers
Actual papers submitted to a professor of English at Cal Poly.

Comments to **Molly Ewing**
Last updated: May 16, 2006. Links checked: May 16, 2006.

Academic Violations Honor Board
ACADEMIC VIOLATIONS: THE HONOR BOARD

A. Philosophy - Academic endeavor is undermined by cheating, plagiarism, or lying for academic advantage. The faculty has the duty to promote an atmosphere of honest learning, first through its own example as a community of scholars, but also through the establishment and support of a system by which students charged with academic wrongdoing can be fairly judged, and if found culpable, held accountable. Such a system should be founded on the following principles:

1. The relationship between student and teacher is essentially a private one, one that should be kept between the two parties whenever possible. Therefore, academic violations can and should be kept between the two parties and resolved to their satisfaction. In cases in which matters cannot be resolved in this way, recourse by either party should be to the Honor Board.

2. In most circumstances, grading is the prerogative of the faculty. However, in cases brought before the Honor Board, all parties are obligated to accept the decision resulting from Honor Board procedure.

3. More severe penalties than a faculty member may assess individually (Penalty F, non-implemented suspension, suspension, expulsion) are the responsibility of the College as a whole, and decisions involving such penalties require the participation of the faculty, the students, and the administration.

4. Board members are expected to disqualify themselves from a hearing panel if potential bias for or against a defendant may give the appearance of a conflict of interest.

5. A fair and independent appeal process is vital to protect student rights and correct abuses.

6. Students have rights and are afforded procedural protection through the Campus Judicial Process. These include: a fair notice of violations; b. the opportunity to be heard with fairness; c. the right to present information and witnesses to support the claim; d. right to be treated with equal fairness and dignity.

7. Consistency requires that a relatively small and fixed group hear and judge Honor Board cases.

8. The Honor Board is not an adversarial system.

9. Since the Honor Board and the Community Judicial and Mediation Board are two related parts of the Campus Judicial System, it is in the interest of

justice that individual Honor Board records be available, upon request, to the chair of the Community Judicial and Mediation Board. The chair of that board will not release the contents of the record to the remaining members unless it has found the student culpable of a violation of the Ferrum College Community Standards and Residence Hall Policies. In that case the Honor Board record, if any, will be used only to help assess a proper sanction.

10. Other than as stated in paragraph 9 above, Honor Board records are for the exclusive use of the Honor Board, are not to be used for any other purpose and are destroyed upon graduation of the student. The exceptions are that in the case of suspension or expulsion the sanctions become a part of the student's judicial record. An additional exception is that the chair of the Honor Board will review the names of the individuals in clubs and organizations to determine if these clubs and organizations have individuals with honor violations as outlined in the Ferrum College Incentive Plan. The names and individuals are to be kept strictly confidential.

B. Jurisdiction - Plagiarism, cheating in academic work, academic misrepresentation and multiple submission of the same work without previous written approval of the instructor(s) are offenses which fall under the jurisdiction of the Ferrum College Honor Board.

1. Cheating - Students must complete all tests and examinations without help from any unauthorized source; they may not use, offer, or solicit unauthorized information, materials, or help without the explicit consent of the professor. Cheating offenses include. but are not limited to, looking at another student's paper, an opened textbook, a notebook, or a "crib" sheet during a test; talking to another student during a test; the sharing of information between students who have taken a test and students who have not; and using or soliciting unauthorized test copies as study aids. The student who knowingly shares information or supplies material to another student has also committed a cheating offense and can be charged under this section. These rules apply to take home exams as well as any other unless the professor explicitly says otherwise. Check with the professors to clarify what is acceptable.

2. Plagiarism - What is plagiarism? Plagiarism, according to The Little, Brown Handbook, 7th ed., is "the presentation of someone else's ideas or words as your own" (578). Plagiarism can be deliberate or accidental. Deliberate plagiarism

includes copying a passage word for word with the intention of omitting the source, or summarizing or paraphrasing another's ideas without indicating where they came from, or submitting someone else's work (for example, a paper) as one's own. Accidental plagiarism includes careless omission of quotation marks around a passage that was copied word for word, or the unintended omission of documentation when summarizing or paraphrasing another's ideas. Both deliberate and accidental plagiarism are serious (578). A student must avoid both kinds of plagiarism. The professor of the course will determine the penalty, the most severe of which may be an F in the course.

Which kinds of information need acknowledgment? The Little, Brown Handbook lists three kinds of sources often used in writing a paper: (1) the writer's own "thoughts and experiences"; (2) "common knowledge, the basic knowledge people share," (such as "major facts of history," popular folk literature with untraceable authors), and "common sense observation"; and (3) " other people's independent material." The third category is the one that requires acknowledgment (580-581).

Which format should students use to document a paper? Students should consult their professor to determine the format (such as MLA, APA, or CBE) of a research paper. They should refer to any standard source recommended by their professor.

3. Academic misrepresentation - Any act of dishonesty committed for academic advantage is academic misrepresentation. Violations include, but are not limited to, lying about reasons for absences or for late work and forging an academic document (a drop/add form, for example).

4. Multiple submission of work - Students may not, without the prior written consent of all instructors involved, submit the same work for credit in two or more courses simultaneously or for a repetition of the same course, nor may they submit previous work completed at Ferrum or at another institution without the prior written consent of the current instructor.

5. Failure to cooperate with the Honor Board - Members of the college community who are notified of Honor Board action which involves them and who fail to attend a scheduled meeting or hearing may be subject to disciplinary action, at the discretion of the Honor Board. Witnesses are required to testify when called. Students

found culpable of an Honor Board violation who fail to comply with the sanction(s) set by the board may be subject to further disciplinary action.

C. Organization - The Honor Board shall hear two types of cases. First, any member of the College community may bring a case directly to the Honor Board. This is called an "initial case". Second, the student involved may appeal to the Honor Board if it is felt that the faculty member's settlement was unfair. This is called an "appeal". Both types of cases shall be heard by an Honor Board panel with student participation and with the right to appeal an Honor Board decision to the Dean of the College or designee. Five members of the faculty shall be nominated to the Honor Board. Each will serve a three-year term. Terms are staggered as prescribed by the Dean of the College. Elections for new members are held during the first regular faculty meeting of the year. The Board shall choose its own chairperson. The chair or chair's designee normally is a non-voting member who shall arrange the time, place and personnel for the hearing panels. The Honor Board chairperson shall keep the files and records of the Honor Board. The Student Government Association Executive Council shall nominate five students to serve on the hearing panels, and they shall be confirmed by the Vice President and Dean of the College. The SGA is required to inform the chairperson of the names, phone numbers, and local addresses of the selected students within 15 days of selection.

D. Process - A faculty member who learns of a possible violation from personal observation, physical evidence, or the complaint of a student may settle this matter privately with the accused student. Once the faculty member is satisfied of the student's culpability, he or she must check with the Honor Board chairperson (1) to be sure of the proper procedure and (2) to be aware of previous infractions (though not the details). If there are any previous violations, the chairperson will urge that the case come to the Honor Board so that the sanction will reflect this history, since the most severe sanction an individual faculty member can give is limited to an F in the course. The faculty member is obligated to inform the student of his or her decision and must report any violation, including those settled privately, to the Honor Board chairperson for the Board's permanent records. This information should include the name of the student involved and the decision on the matter. A form for this purpose is available from the Honor Board chair or the Dean's Office. The faculty member is also required to advise the student of the right to appeal this decision to the Honor Board within two working days. The faculty member must inform the student of the name, phone number, and office location of the chairperson. If the faculty member considers appropriate a penalty more severe than an F in the course, then the faculty member must bring the case directly to the Honor Board. The Honor Board shall handle this case according to its initial case procedure.

Plagiarism

"I found your speech to be good and original. However, the part that was original was not good. And the part that was good was not original."
-Samuel Johnson, to one of his less motivated students

What is plagiarism?

First and foremost, plagiarism is a **crime**. It is the theft of intellectual property. Plagiarism can lead to legal action against you or the College for copyright violations.

Plagiarism is defined as the use of another author's words, research, or ideas without proper attribution and citation, whether such use is *intentional* or *unintentional*.

Examples of plagiarism:

- Word-for-word copying from a source, without quotation marks and without attribution and citation of the original source.

- Paraphrasing or summarizing a source in your own words, without attribution or citation of the original source.

- Use of any factual information (that is not considered common knowledge), statistics, photographs, charts, etc. without attribution and citation of the original source.

What is considered "common knowledge"?

"Common knowledge" may be defined as any factual information that can be presumed to be known by most people with average education - "George Washington was our first President", or which can be found in multiple (more than 5 sources). Use the "look it up" rule: if you need to look up factual information for verification, it should not be considered common knowledge and should be cited.

Why shouldn't I plagiarize?

- You will get caught. There are multiple techniques and tools available to your professors to detect plagiarism.

- It is unethical and dishonest.

- It is a criminal act which can lead to legal action.

- You will devalue your diploma if Hanover College develops a reputation for academic dishonesty.

For more information

Hanover College Policy on Academic Dishonesty: http://www.hanover.edu/registrar/honest.htm

Indiana University Writing Center's excellent tutorial on avoiding plagiarism:
http://www.indiana.edu/~wts/wts/plagiarism.html

http://www.nwmissouri.edu/library/services/facplag.htm: From the Northwest Missouri State
University Library web site, provides links for prevention strategies for faculty, tips on avoiding
plagiarism for students, and how to diagnose plagiarism if suspected.

http://www.web-miner.com/plagiarism: A meta-site containing numerous links to online articles and
other plagiarism resources for instructors (for example, how to think and talk about plagiarism in the
classroom) and students (such as avoiding plagiarism).

updated 7 August 2006

Lake Forest College Statement on Academic Honesty and Plagiarism

Plagiarism is "the unauthorized use or close imitation of the language and thoughts of another author and the representation of them as one's own original work" (*Random House Compact Unabridged Dictionary,* 1997).

Most people recognize the more obvious forms of plagiarism — copying another student's test paper, buying a research paper, or copying material directly out of published work — but there are less blatant forms of plagiarism which sometimes result from a writer's unintentional misuse of source materials. You may have plagiarized without realizing what you have done, but being unaware does not justify or excuse plagiarism. The following guidelines will help you to give correct credit to your sources.

KEEP THESE PRINCIPLES IN MIND

- **Quoting:** If you use another person's words, enclose them in quotation marks and document the source in a footnote, endnote, or parentheses (depending on the style of documentation required for your paper).
- **Paraphrasing:** When you restate another person's idea in your own words, you are paraphrasing. Unless you cite a source, your reader will assume that the wording is entirely your own. Since a paraphrase is based on another person's idea, its source must always be documented.
- **Common knowledge:** Many people are aware that common knowledge — factual material such as dates or scientific formulae — need not be documented. If you are unsure if a given fact is common knowledge, cite its source. It is better to be cautious and thorough than to risk plagiarism.
- **Cutting and pasting:** It is very easy to cut and paste material from one electronic document to another, for example, from a Web site to a term paper. Take care to note with quotation marks when you have cut and pasted material, and document all pasted passages as you would any quotation.
- **Downloading:** Any information that you download from the Web, databases, or other electronic resources and use in a paper must be properly cited. Remember to use quotation marks around any downloaded text that you incorporate into your paper.

IMPORTANT TERMS

- **Bibliography or Works Cited:** In the case of a paper, these terms refer to a list of books, articles, Web sites, interviews, music, films, and other documents quoted or paraphrased. These vary in format based on style (examples are MLA, APA, Chicago Manual of Style). Providing a bibliography or a list of works cited is one way to document your sources. This list will usually appear as the last page of your paper.
- **Cite:** To quote directly, to paraphrase, and to document the source. There are several citation styles.
- **Footnotes and Endnotes:** These are ways of documenting your citations. Footnotes appear at the bottom of each page of your paper and refer to citations on that page. Endnotes appear at the end of the paper's text. The requirements for footnotes and endnotes vary by citation style. Check with your professor or the Writing Center for more information.

EXAMPLES

The examples of plagiarism below are based on the following quotation:

> Most fairy tales originated in periods when religion was a most important part of life; thus they deal, directly or by inference, with religious themes. The stories of *The Thousand and One Nights* are full of references to Islamic religion. A great many Western fairy tales have religious content; but most of these stories are neglected today and unknown to the larger public just because, for many, these religious themes no longer arouse universally and personally meaningful associations. Bruno Bettelheim, *The Uses Of Enchantment* (New York: Vintage Books, 1976, 13).

A. If you use part of the language of the passage, put quotation marks around the borrowed words and cite the source.

Incorrect:

People today find that religious themes no longer arouse universally and personally meaningful associations.

Correct:

People today find that "religious themes no longer arouse universally and personally meaningful associations."[1]

B. If you paraphrase the original, be sure to document the source of the borrowed idea.

Incorrect:

According to Bruno Bettelheim, some fairy tales are ignored because people no longer seem to respond to their religious themes.

Correct:

According to Bruno Bettelheim, some fairy tales are ignored because people no longer seem to respond to their religious themes.[1]

C. If you use an idea based on a point made by another person, you must acknowledge your source.

Incorrect:

The stories from *The Thousand and One Nights* which deal with Islamic religion are not likely to be popular with modern Americans.

Correct:

The stories from *The Thousand and One Nights* which deal with Islamic religion are not likely to be popular with modern Americans.[1]

Correct:

According to Bettelheim's theories about fairy tales and religion, the stories from *The Thousand and One Nights* which deal with Islamic religion are not likely to be popular with modern Americans.[1]

FURTHER INFORMATION

Information on the format of quotations and footnotes may be found in many reference books. One standard reference is *A Pocket Style Manual,* 2nd ed. by Diana Hacker. For information on citing electronic sources, see "Citing Electronic Resources" on the Lake Forest College library Web page at http://www.lib.lfc.edu/

Lake Forest College is committed to the ideals of academic honesty as outlined in the *Lake Forest College Student Handbook.*

Approved by the Dean of the Faculty, July 1999

"This Internet is great for research. I think my report on California breaks a Guinness World Record. 174.513 separate sources!"

Credit for this cartoon must be given to <u>Jerry's Web site</u> (http://www.jerryking.com/) and to **From Now On** (http://fno.org),
The Educational Technology Journal.

PLAGIARISM: ADVICE FOR STUDENTS

As our hero shows us in the cartoon above, the Internet has really changed the way students do research. It gives students access to tons of material from a wide array of sources. And it is easy access -- a click here, a click there. In the past, it was more difficult to do research and more difficult to use the work of others. Today the very ease in which students can access electronic material can be a source of great temptation. The ability to "cut and paste" from a variety of authors without ever citing the source is a variant of an old problem called **plagiarism**, a serious offense in the academic community. Electronic information didn't create the problem of plagiarism. It has been around for a long time. And you don't need a computer to commit plagiarism today either. It just has made the opportunity to use another's work as if it were one's own more tempting. If the proud fellow in this cartoon had cited the sources he is boasting that he has taken from the Internet, it's not at all clear that he would have been able physically to even pull the load of paper he would have created. Developing the skill of proper **citation of sources** is the student's best way of avoiding ever being charged with this serious offense.

DEFINING PLAGIARISM:
The issue of plagiarism goes right to the heart of the academic experience. One must credit the work of another. To do otherwise is to commit intellectual theft and the penalties can be severe.

"To use another person's ideas or expressions in your writing without acknowledging the source is to plagiarize. Plagiarism, then, constitutes intellectual theft." This definition is taken from the *MLA Handbook for Writers of Research Papers 5th ed.* The book is concerned about helping students and other writers to improve their ability to **cite sources** properly. It is concerned with only one style of citation, MLA format, but there are a number of other styles, such as APA, Chicago Style, and Turabian. Your instructor determines the style you must use. However, whichever style you use, **it is the proper use of citation styles that gives the most protection against the offense of plagiarism.**

TYPES OF PLAGIARISM:

Most students are familiar with the concept of intentional plagiarism, involving a direct copying of another's work in one form or another. However, **there are many more subtle ways of using another's work, which are also considered to be plagiarism**. It is the college student's responsibility to understand these. When in doubt, ask a librarian or the appropriate faculty member for advice.

Intentional

- To copy a work, or part of a work directly from a source, word for word, without citing it.
- To submit a paper written by another student.
- To intersperse the words of another within your work without giving credit.

Unintentional

- Recognition of even apt phrases or clever wording, through parenthetical documentation, must be given.
- The reworking of a paper submitted for another course must have the current instructor's permission.
- Collaborative work on a paper must be clearly acknowledged.

While it is the student's responsibility to give proper credit to the work of others when producing a term paper, thesis, etc., the faculty and librarians of the College are available to assist with any questions you may have on the topic.

The *MLA Handbook for Writers of Research Papers, 5th ed.,* section 1.8, pp. 30-34, gives a detailed discussion and important examples of plagiarism. The Call No. of this book, which is on reserve in the Library, is **REF LB 2369 .G53 1999.**

PENALTIES FOR PLAGIARISM

At Manhattanville College the Student Handbook (see pp. 47-48) lists **plagiarism** as a form of Academic Dishonesty. Procedures for reporting instances of plagiarism are discussed there and a range of penalties, **including dismissal and expulsion**, are listed. A judicial procedure for dealing with cases of suspected plagiarism brought by instructors is spelled out also. The class ERes page has a copy of the Manhattanville College policy entitled, "Academic Conduct and Adjudication" for more detailed information.

CITATION - THE BEST DEFENSE

There are a number of citation styles used by the academic community to deal with the proper recognition of another's work. A student must use the citation style called by his/her instructor. For the most part certain subjects use certain citation styles. For example, most students of education use APA (American Psychological Association) style.

Also, the Library website maintains examples of two of the major citation styles, APA and MLA. Go to the Library Home Page and look under *Courses and Tutorials* for the latest information.

In addition to the *MLA Handbook for Writers of Research Papers, 5th ed.* mentioned earlier, books which describe and give examples of the major citation styles are on Reserve at the Circulation Desk. The titles and Call Numbers follow:

> *The Bluebook: A Uniform System of Citation/ compiled by the editors of The Columbia Law Review, the Harvard Law Review, the University Pennsylvania Law Review and the Yale Law Journal, 15th ed.,1991.*
> **REF KF245. U5 1991**.

> *Publication Manual of the American Psychological Association, 4th ed., 2001.*
> **REF BF76.7 .P83 2001**

> *The Chicago Manual of Style, 1993*
> **REF Z253 . U69 1993**

> *Turabian, Kate L. A Manual for Writers of Term Papers, Theses, and Dissertation. 1996*
> **LB2369 . T8 1996**

Avoiding Plagiarism

What is Plagiarism?

The *American Heritage Dictionary, Fourth Edition*, defines the verb plagiarize as "to use and pass off (the ideas or writings of another) as one's own" or "to appropriate for use as one's own passages or ideas from (another). The Latin root of plagiarize is *plagiarius* which means kidnapper.

Plagiarism is also addressed in the College Catalog which states that

"anything that is written in a paper, book report, or any other assignment must be in the student's own words or must properly and fully indicate the source(s). Anything that students copy word for word from another source is a direct quotation. All direct quotations must be shown as such and must be properly documented. Students must also rewrite paraphrased material in a style and language that are distinctively their own; merely rearranging the words found in a scholarly source is plagiarism."

For more information on this, please consult the College Catalog or your academic advisor.

Ways to Avoid Plagiarism When Using Library Resources

- Pick a topic that interests you! It will be easier to understand others' thoughts and integrate (not just insert) them into your paper.
- Start your research early - you will produce a better paper and spend more time on your work when you're not under pressure.
- When you are making photocopies, always remember to write down where you got your information, so you will not be tempted later to make up the citation.
- Take notes from a book or journal article using keywords rather than whole phrases or sentences from the original. This will make it easier for you to put the ideas into your own words. Copy down the citation information for the source and include it in your bibliography.
- If you can't find a way to paraphrase the information, quote directly from the material giving the correct citation to the original. Check with your instructor to make sure that quoting is permitted first.

- If you're not certain that you're paraphrasing instead of plagiarizing, have an advisor or instructor take a look at a draft of your paper.

Also:

If your professor has enrolled your class in <u>Turn-It-In</u>, the anti-plagiarism software, you will want to know how to open your account and submit assignments. For information on using Turn-It-In, go to the library's <u>Turn-It-In Student Guide</u>. For assistance with Turn-It-In please contact the Davis Memorial Library Reference Desk at (910) 630-7123.

Preventing and Detecting Plagiarism: a faculty workshop

Holly Heller-Ross, Associate Librarian

This introductory workshop focuses on using new strategies and information technologies to assist faculty in preventing and detecting plagiarism. What are the common clues, and what can faculty do when we suspect plagiarism? We can search the Internet for suspect phrases, but there's a lot more we can do as well. Combining strategies such as requiring specific research steps and working bibliographies with a wider range of detection tools than a simple web search can improve faculty ability to both prevent plagiarism and detect it more easily should it occur.

"Internet plagiarism is a growing concern on all campuses as students struggle to understand what constitutes acceptable use of the Internet. In the absence of clear direction from faculty, most students have concluded that 'cut & paste' plagiarism - using a sentence or two (or more) from different sources on the Internet and weaving this information together into a paper without appropriate citation - is not a serious issue. While 10% of students admitted to engaging in such behavior in 1999, this rose to 41% in a 2001 survey with the majority of students (68%) suggesting this was not a serious issue".
Center for Academic Integrity http://www.academicintegrity.org/cai_research.asp

Plattsburgh State University Policy

Academic Honesty and Cut & Paste Plagiarism

Tutorials and Teaching Resources

Plagiarism Detection
Assignment Strategies for Reducing Plagiarism

Citation Help and Citation Format Online Guides

General Information about Electronic Plagiarism

General Information about Electronic Plagiarism

>   "Paper Mills"

>   Sites Regarding Copyright, Especially for Educators

See also (in Feinberg Library):

PN 167 Harris, Robert A., and Vic Lockman. The Plagiarism Handbook: Strategies for
.H37   Preventing, Detecting, and Dealing with Plagiarism. Los Angeles: Pyrczak, 2001.
2001   Website : www.virtualsalt.com/antiplag.htm

Plattsburgh State University Policy

"Academic honesty is essential to the intellectual health of the university and the ideals of education. SUNY Plattsburgh expects students to be honest and to conduct themselves with integrity in all aspects of their relationship with the college (e.g., application, transfer evaluation, academic progress review, and credit and non-credit bearing experiences, including regular course work, independent studies, internships, practica, student teaching, and interactions with faculty, staff, and students). Academic dishonesty adversely affects the educational function of the college and undermines the integrity of its programs.

Dishonest conduct includes, but is not limited to, cheating, plagiarism, unauthorized collaboration, forgery, and alteration of records, along with any lying, deceit, bribery, coercion, or intimidation for the purpose of influencing a grade or for any other academic gain. Action against a student determined to have violated the academic honesty policy can range from a reduction of the grade on an assignment, through failure of a course, to suspension or even dismissal from the academic program, the department, or the college.

A student who is charged with academic dishonesty will be afforded due process through the College Judicial System. (See Procedures for Addressing Suspected Academic Dishonesty.)"

Plattsburgh State Policies: Cheating

Academic Honesty and Cut & Paste Plagiarism

Combating Plagiarism. by Brian Hansen, from the CQ Researcher, September 19, 2003, provides an excellent and well documented report on plagiarism including recent newsworthy cases, an historical timeline, and a pro/con essay on Turnitin.com. It's a PDF file, about 24 pages.

Legal Aspects of Academic Dishonesty by Dennis Bricault 1998, provides a summary of legal issues and cases, a literature review, and the results of his research at North Park University.

Plagiarism and Ethics by Holly Heller-Ross, a simplified one-page review of major western ethical theories and their application to the problem of plagiarism.

Plagiarism in Colleges in USA by attorney Ronald B. Standler 2000, provides a review of legal cases involving education law and plagiarism.

Why do students cheat? (NPR's "All Things Considered" report on cheating--RealPlayer needed) Students are able to copy and paste from Web sites and full-text articles and book chapters into word processed drafts of their papers. Many mistakenly think that all information on the Internet is free, and this makes it perfectly legal and acceptable to use it without attribution. In addition, citation formats for Web sites can be difficult. A thorough discussion of student motivation can be found at the "Academic Dishonesty" location on Wesleyan University Library's page on Turnitin. (See Turnitin.com below for URL.)

Some online information companies provide students, for a subscription fee, to search for their topics in virtual libraries owned by the providers. Look at Questia, for example. For $19.95 monthly a student can copy text and paste it into a paper and Questia will provide a bibliographic citation--in the selected correct format (e.g., APA, MLA). Some librarians teach how to copy and paste as part of the services their libraries offer; while they certainly address the question of attribution, students may remember more of the skills and less of the intellectual content of such workshops.

The library journal College & Research Libraries News (C&RL News) published an Internet resource guide by librarian Patience Simmonds in June of 2003 to Plagiarism and Cyber-Plagiarism with current links to plagiarism awareness sites, honor codes, detection tools, online seminars, and paper mills. C&RL News now maintains the resource guide on their web site.

Students are not skilled in paraphrasing and often need practice. **Some online examples of paraphrasing for students** include:

Do You Use the Words of Others or Your Own Words?
<www.acts.twu.ca/lbr/research_essays2.htm#words> Bill Badke, a librarian at Trinity Western University in Langley, British Columbia, gives easy to understand advice about paraphrasing.

Avoiding Plagiarism from Hamilton College
<http://www.hamilton.edu/academic/Resource/WC/AvoidingPlagiarism.html> A text explanation with examples of poor paraphrases. (Author's permission to use, always citing Hamilton College as the source.)

Avoiding Plagiarism from Purdue University's Writing Lab
<http://owl.english.purdue.edu/handouts/research/r_plagiar.html> Attractively formatted for printing as a handout for students with examples and advice about paraphrasing. Please note the "Terms and Conditions of Fair Use" of this page.

Avoiding Plagiarism from DePauw University Writing Center
<http://www.depauw.edu/admin/arc/writing_center/plagiarism.htm> Another well formatted page with examples of proper and improper paraphrasing. (Author's permission received for this link.)

Exercise on Citation and Paraphrase from California Lutheran University
<http://web.grinnell.edu/writinglab/CitationGuides/Indivex.html> An **exercise** that shows students various ways to quote and paraphrase work. (Author's permission received for this link.)

Tutorials and Teaching Resources

Plagiarism 101 from SUNY Albany
Subtitled: How to write term papers without being sucked into the black hole.
<http://library.albany.edu/usered/plagiarism/index.html> A introductory tutorial with information, "what would you do?" scenarios, and a self-quiz.

Plagiarism Tutorial from North Carolina State University
<http://www.lib.ncsu.edu/scc/tutorial/plagiarism/index.html> Developed by the NCSU Libraries' Scholarly Communication Center, this tutorial covers definitions, rules and regulations.

Searchpath Module 6: Citing Sources from Western Michigan University
<http://www.wmich.edu/library/searchpath/mod6/index.html> This module of the
Searchpath information literacy tutorial includes interactive exercises on citations and
avoiding plagiarism. It also provides a quiz.

Straight Talk about Plagiarism from Bedford/St. Martins
This two page handout in PDF format developed by publisher Bedford/St.Martins can be
distributed freely to students.

The Bedford/St. Martins Workshop on Plagiarism provides information on use of portfolios
and reviews online detection tools.

Plagiarism and Online Paper Mills from Plattsburgh State University
<http://www2.plattsburgh.edu/instruct/iu/plagiarism.htm >This Feinberg Library resource
page provides resource links for Plattsburgh faculty to use in teaching and planning course
assignments.

Plagiarism Detection

Reference Sources and Circulating Books
Students may find ready-made essays, descriptions, and analysis in paper library reference
sources as well as in online sources. Faculty familiarity with these sources will provide an
intuitive sense of when checking a reference source for possible plagiarized text would be
useful. Library Liaisons can help keep faculty up-to-date as new reference materials are
added to the library shelves. While no-one can be expected to memorize the content of all the
circulating books in their area, a quick library catalog search on a topic could lead to possible
sources of plagiarized or improperly cited material.

Full-text Online Databases
Students use full-text research databases at an ever-increasing rate. Journal articles and book
chapters found in these databases are not included in web search engine results, as they are
part of the "invisible web". Faculty familiarity with the journals in their disciplines that are
part of the library's full-text databases will make detecting plagiarism for these sources a
little easier. Feinberg subscribes to over 17 full-text databases, covering thousands of
journals.

Search Engines

Students find pre-written academic papers by using search engines; almost any search engine
will return information about papers to buy or download at no charge. A simple search under
the topic of a paper, combined with a phrase such as "free papers" or "term paper" will
retrieve numerous sites. Examples of some commonly used search engines include:

Google: Students can find papers using Google's Directory. There is a link under
Directory/Reference/Education/Products and Services/Academic Papers. This is subdivided
into "Fee based" and "Free." There are 39 sites listed as sources for free papers and 30 sites
where students are able to purchase papers.

Ask Jeeves: A subject search identical to that used in Google resulted in a list of 29 sites for
free papers and 20 will provide papers for a fee.

<u>Yahoo!</u>: A search under *charlemagne +"term paper"* resulted in 419 hits, some free paper sites, some fee-based paper sites, some assignment descriptions from course syllabi.

Faculty may use the same search engines and very similar techniques to scan for suspicious phrases. Meta-engines such as <u>Meta-Crawler</u> also may be used successfully for such searches.

Commercial Services

Some institutions subscribe to commercial detection services. Individual faculty members also may subscribe to such services.

<u>Turnitin.com</u> - The first sentence on the Home page for this service states that it is "the world's leading plagiarism prevention system." Individual subscriptions are available. A Web page created by Wesleyan University librarian Kendall Hobbs provides a good overview of this service. See "<u>Plagiarism and Turnitin.com</u>" <<u>http://www.wesleyan.edu/libr/turnitin/</u>>
Look at a <u>sample document</u>

<u>CiteMaster</u> - Its Home page states that it is "a learning tool for both students and educators." A press release about the service reads: "Through the use of customized algorithms, CiteMaster performs a unique text-to-text comparison of a submitted paper with a database consisting of primary and secondary materials. Our proprietary three-stage approach allows CiteMaster to find both exact and reasonably inexact text matches with a high degree of accuracy and speed. CiteMaster presently performs potential plagiarism/citation searches on a database of more than 2 million essays downloaded from the Internet aimed at highschool [*sic*] students and college undergraduates." <http://www.citemaster.com>

<u>Glatt Plagiarism Screening Program</u> - A service that will blank words on a submitted paper so that an instructor can ask the student to fill in the blanks. The company also offers a "computer-assisted" teaching program to help students learn to paraphrase. <http://www.plagiarism.com/screen.id.htm>

<u>EduTie.com</u> - Free Trial includes 10 free submissions of student papers. <http://www.edutie.com/> (Thanks to Jose de Ondarza for submitting this link.)

<u>Plagiarism.org</u> - Links to Turnitin.com (above). Offers a free trial for 5 papers/reports (1 month limit). <http://www.plagiarism.org/> (Thanks to Jose de Ondarza for submitting this link.)

<u>EVE2</u> - Essay Verification Engine, a downloadable program with free 15-day trial <http://www.canexus.com/eve/index.shtml> (Thanks to Jose de Ondarza for submitting this link.)

Assignment Strategies for Reducing Plagiarism

Annotated Bibliography: Involves use of a stated number of sources. Describe each source-- in three to five sentences only--as to its relevance and value to the topic. Include a source that was NOT helpful or would make it as a "runner-up."

- Do not require a laundry list of, for example, 3 journal articles, 1 Web site, and 2 books Not all topics are covered equally well in all information formats

- Require that all Web sites have identifiable authors, either persons or organizations/corporate bodies

- Make sure students know that a periodical article from a subscription full-text database is not considered a "Web site"

Working Bibliographies: Requires submission of a working bibliographies weeks before the paper is due. The working bibliography must include more sources than would likely be needed for the paper, e.g., 10 items for a 5-page paper.

- Include notes indicating any materials have been requested through Interlibrary Loan

- Annotate each item for only particular characteristics, e.g., timeliness or technicality

- Use proper citation format

Literature Review (or update an older literature review): Involves discovering how a topic evolves in your field.

- Learn what a literature review is and its usefulness to scholars

- Use indexes (not only online) to locate reviews

- Trace the evolution of a topic

Segmented or Serial Reports: Require that students work on one topic throughout the semester with pieces of their research turned in periodically. An example is a complete study of homelessness that includes individual brief submissions such as: Basic Overview, including separate aspects that could be researched; Current Controversies/Areas of Interest; Historical Background of one aspect; Examples of Solutions, including both documented and speculative approaches.

- Students may all use the same topic for such long term projects.

- Topics and aspects will require use of different information sources.

Personal Reflection: Require students to reflect on how the topics relate to their lives, academic goals, social situations/backgrounds.

(Some ideas in this section were suggested by Wesleyan University librarian Kendall Hobbs and the Web site on plagiarism at Lemoyne College <http://www.lemoyne.edu/library/plagiarism.htm#PREVENTING PLAGIARISM>)

More Ideas for Alternatives to Research Papers: See the Columbia Gorge Community College page on Alternatives to Term Papers This is an excellent source for ideas.
http://www.cgcc.cc.or.us/Library/alternatives.htm

Citation Help and Citation Format Online Guides

The Feinberg Library at Plattsburgh State will post Web pages to help students with citation formats. Currently that information is available through a link, "How to Cite Sources," on the Research Resources page <http://www2.plattsburgh.edu/instruct/iu/researchhelp.htm>

Professional associations' formatting help:

- American Psychological Association--**APA**: http://www.apastyle.org/

- Modern Language Association--**MLA**: http://www.mla.org/ (Click on *MLA Style*)

- Council of Science Editors--formerly **CBE**: http://www.councilscienceeditors.org/pubs_ssf_7th.shtml (This is a link to new information that will be included in the forthcoming 7th edition of the organization's style manual.)

- Chicago Manual of Style (also "Turabian"): http://www.press.uchicago.edu/Misc/Chicago/cmosfaq/cmosfaq.htoc.html

- American Chemical Society--**ACS**: http://chemistry.org/portal/Chemistry?PID=acsdisplay.html&DOC=library%5Csciwriting.html This page links to other pages with guides.

General Information about Electronic Plagiarism

"Paper mills"

There is a good collection of approximately 150 sites at the Web site, "Internet Paper Mills," <www.coastal.edu/library/mills2.htm> It was created by Margaret Fain, a librarian at Coastal Carolina University. The page was last updated in March 2002, and a random check of links indicated that they are still good.

Sites regarding copyright, especially for educators

Fair Use Harbor <www.stfrancis.edu/cid/copyrightbay/> A tutorial for all who have questions about copyright, what it allows and doesn't allow, especially regarding "fair use."

Crash Course in Copyright <www.utsystem.edu/ogc/intellectualproperty/cprtindx.htm#top> University of Texas tutorial on copyright.

10 Big Myths about copyright explained <www.templetons.com/brad/copymyths.html> A straightforward approach to copyright by the Chairman of the Board of the Electronic Frontier Foundation, "the leading foundation protecting liberties and privacy in cyberspace."

Copyright Law: Using Information Legally <www.library.jhu.edu/elp/useit/copyright/index.html> Johns Hopkins University Q&A-links page on copyright.

©Primer from the Center for Intellectual Property and Copyright, University of Maryland University College <http://www.umuc.edu/cgi-bin/cgiwrap/primer/primerwrap.cgi/enter.php> "[A]n online, interactive tutorial on copyright basics called the ©Primer. The Primer is a free interactive online tool to assist educating faculty, staff and students about copyright principles and compliance." (Description from a news release.)

This page created by Carla List-Handley. C2000

Revised and Updated by Holly Heller-Ross

Last updated: 16 Mar 2005

Detecting Electronic Plagiarism for Suffolk University Faculty

Electronic information resources have made it easier for students to conduct research. The Sawyer Library subscribes to dozens of databases with literally millions of articles in full text. Students can also use search engines on the World Wide Web to find completed papers from millions of Internet sites. It has become easy to manage blocks of text using download, copy and paste commands through the computer workstation's operating system (Windows or Mac). To further complicate matters, there are almost one hundred known paper mills on the Internet for students willing to pay for completed papers.

Service for Suffolk University Faculty to Help Detect Plagiarism

CAS Academic Computing has acquired Turnitin (http://www.turnitin.com), a software program that scans student papers for incidences of plagiarism. According to Turnitin's documentation:

> We prevent and detect plagiarism by comparing submitted papers to billions of pages of content located on the Internet and our proprietary databases. The results of our comparisons are compiled, one for each paper submitted, in custom "Originality Reports." These reports are sent to participating educators, who access the results by logging into their Turnitin account(s).

For more information on this program, please visit Turnitin or contact CAS Academic Computing.

Guides

- Suffolk University Professor Gerry Richman in the English Department has prepared an excellent, Web-accessible guide entitled "Detecting Electronic Plagiarism."
- Ronald B. Standler, Ph.D., former Associate Professor of Electrical Engineering at The Pennsylvania State University and now a Massachusetts lawyer has written Plagiarism in Colleges in USA, an essay discussing plagiarism from a legal perspective for students as well as faculty.

The Sawyer Library's Subscription Databases

Plagiarism is not necessarily content from Internet sites; it is just as easy to plagiarize using the millions of articles available through the thousands of full-text journals accessible and available through the databases licensed by the Sawyer Library.

It is possible to detect plagiarism involving the library's subscription databases:

- check the bibliographies and footnotes provided by the student

- conduct a search through our databases using keywords from the paper. Many of the library's <u>databases are subject-based rather than general</u>; you will not have to check all of the databases when searching for content.
- ask us for help; we will make every effort to assist faculty in detecting plagiarism.

Using an Internet Search Engine for Detecting Plagiarism

Faculty members can use an Internet search engine to help find copied works. Use a "search engine" (such as Google) rather than a "search directory" (such as Yahoo!) because a search engine indexes almost every word at a web site for its database, whereas a search directory categorizes an entire site into subject areas and individual words may or may not be indexed.

How to:

- it is recommended you look for a unique <u>four or five word exact phrase</u> as it appears in the paper
- type the phrase into the search engine surrounded by quotation marks
- for example, "extent of gender wage discrimination"

Google found **four hits. The advantage of Google is that it highlights (by bolding) the phrase in the search results,** facilitating review.

Searched the web for **"extent of gender wage discrimination"**.

Regional Economist -- Economic Background Article
... man. Many believe that the **wage** gap is a good measure of the **extent** of **gender wage discrimination**, which occurs when men and women are not paid equal wages for ...
www.stls.frb.org/publications/re/2000/d/pages/economic-backgnd.html - 23k - Cached - Similar pa

Economic Education - Inside the Vault
... are not paid equal wages for substantially equal work. Many people believe that the **wage** gap is a good measure of the **extent** of **gender wage discrimination**. ...
www.stls.frb.org/publications/itv/2001/a/pages/q-a.html - 13k - Cached - Similar pages

[PDF] www.iza.org/espe2000/papers/gardeazabal_ugidos.pdf
File Format: PDF/Adobe Acrobat - View as Text
... in the returns to these endowments. The latter part is then used to calculate the **extent** of **gender wage discrimination**. Oaxaca's measure of **discrimination** is a ...
Similar pages

[PDF] 198.252.9.108/govper/InsideVault/www.stls.frb.org/publications/itv/2001a.pdf
File Format: PDF/Adobe Acrobat - View as Text
... wages for substantially equal work. Many people believe that the **wage** gap is a good measure of the **extent** of **gender wage discrimination**. Q. Has this **wage** gap ...

Hotbot returned **one hit.**

Recommended search engines:
- Google (http://www.google.com/)
- HotBot (http://www.hotbot.com/Default.asp)

Internet Paper Mills

There are nearly 100 Internet paper mills throughout the world used by students. These are a few of the largest that also advertise directly to students:

- Research papers Online
- FastPapers.com
- Cheathouse.com

An excellent list of "Cheating 101: Internet Paper Mills" is maintained by Margaret Fain, Library Instruction Coordinator, Kimbel Library, Coastal Carolina University.

What is plagiarism?

Plagiarism, strictly speaking, is the stealing of words, ideas, images, or creative works. Plagiarism, whether or not it is intentional, is looked upon as an academic crime.

Copyright violation is closely related to plagiarism, but it is a federal crime (U.S. Copyright Act 17 U.S.C. §§ 101 - 810). Copyright laws protect the rights of creators of any literary, graphic, musical, artistic, or electronic form. (Facts and ideas are not covered, only the expression of those facts or ideas fixed in a tangible form.) The laws, in effect, keep the right to copy those forms in the hands of the people who created them.

College students often are asked to synthesize what they read. From this synthesis often springs a research paper or project, one that cites sources and offers insight to the information. Sounds easy enough, but what happens when students consult multiple sources, learning a little from each one, is that the information becomes muddled, and the students don't always cite facts properly - plagiarism.

Some students think it's difficult to improve on what a professional writer says, so the writer's words end up in the paper, presentation, or project, either quoted extensively, or with a few words changed to avoid direct quotes - also plagiarism.

Other students ask friends for help, which can lead to plagiarism. And some end up with bad information from poor sources, or, worse yet, copy and paste willy-nilly from Internet sites - plagiarism again.

Writing for the Web can be even more problematic, leading to copyright law violations. **When students capture images or text from other websites or scan hard copy to include in a website without attribution or permission, the result can be a violation of copyright law.**

The University of Maine at Farmington Code of Academic Integrity clearly defines plagiarism and other academic integrity violations.

Who cares?

The University of Maine at Farmington is a community of learners. We come together to learn from and to teach each other. Inherent in that relationship is an expectation of academic integrity, an ethic of scholarship. The **Code of Academic Integrity** is an integral part of this campus. While UMF places a high value on academic freedom and the rights of faculty members to employ whatever teaching strategies they deem appropriate, we members of this academic community agree on one point: we share in the responsibilities of making UMF a place of academic integrity. **Students are expected to educate themselves about ethical standards and seek advice when they have questions about academic integrity.**

Because we understand that

- the University of Maine at Farmington is a community of learners,
- every individual's role in this community is valued, and
- the community is damaged when its members do not uphold academic integrity,

we pledge to protect our community by abiding by the Code of Academic Integrity.

The **University of Maine at Farmington Code of Academic Integrity** emphasizes the need for commitment to academic integrity in its <u>introduction</u>.

Why is plagiarism difficult to avoid?

Some cases of plagiarism are blatant. The 2003 revelation that a *New York Times* reporter had stolen and made up stories threatened to bring down one of the world's most famous newspapers. By the time the investigation into Jayson Blair's career had unfolded, the *Times* had been embarrassed to the point that Executive Editor Howell Raines and Managing Editor Gerald Boyd had resigned. Because journalism, like academics, is built on trust, the entire field faced a credibility crisis. Plagiarism cases like this one are difficult to defend.

At other times, plagiarism is a sticky subject, one that gets students and even professional writers into trouble from time to time. What's so sticky about it? Well, the experts don't always agree on what is or isn't plagiarism. For example, two noted historians, Stephen Ambrose in 2001 and Doris Kearns Goodwin in 2002, got into trouble even though their works used footnotes clearly indicating their sources. The problems lay in sentence structures that too closely mirrored the original texts. So, you see, even **citing your sources may not be enough to avoid an accusation of plagiarism**.

Even though scholars aren't always sure how to define plagiarism, they usually know it when they see it. When they see it, their first reaction is to assume the plagiarism is intentional (as much as all of us like to believe the best about our fellow human beings). Frankly, whether the act is intentional or not is often beside the point.

If you have questions about plagiarism, it's better to ask your professor or instructor than to guess. Ignorance is not worth the <u>possible penalties</u>. The best way to avoid plagiarism is to do what educators expect: learn something from your writing process. Look for valid and credible sources. Take careful notes. Digest the information. Cite everything that isn't original.

Definite don'ts

- copying and pasting complete papers from electronic sources

- copying and pasting passages from electronic sources without placing the passages in quotes and properly citing the source

- having others write complete papers or portions of papers for you

- summarizing ideas without citing their source

- pulling out quotes from sources without putting quotation marks around the passages

- closely paraphrasing - not putting the information in your own words (even if it's cited)

- quoting statistics without naming the source unless you gathered the data yourself

- using words and passages you don't understand and can't explain

- self-plagiarizing - using one paper for more than one class without the permission of your professors

- making up sources

- making up bibliographic or citation information (page numbers, etc.)

- using photographs, video, or audio without permission or acknowledgment

- translating from one language to another without properly citing the original source

- copying computer programs or other technical information without acknowledgment

- failing to acknowledge sources of oral presentation, slides, or Web projects

- failing to acknowledge sources of elements of nonverbal work: painting, dance, musical composition, mathematical proof

Giving Credit - Papers

When you incorporate someone else's work (words, statistics, charts, graphs, images, etc.) into a paper you are writing, it is extremely important to give credit where credit is due.

Why? First of all, it is just common courtesy. If you have used someone else's work, the least you can do is offer thanks by acknowledging him/her. In addition to courtesy, giving credit will help you to avoid plagiarizing. **Using someone's else's ideas, words, or other creations without clearly acknowledging where they came from is plagiarism.** (It may also be an infringement of copyright. While plagiarism is unethical, infringing copyright is illegal. For more information on copyright, see the What's the deal with the © ? section of this tutorial.)

To avoid plagiarizing, you must give credit whenever you use any piece of information that is not <u>common knowledge</u>.   This includes

- the words, ideas, opinions, or theories of others whether quoted, summarized or paraphrased (For more information, see the <u>Quoting, paraphrasing, and summarizing</u> section of this tutorial.)

- facts, statistics, graphs, charts, images, etc. generated/created by someone other than you

When writing research papers, documented essays, etc. you give credit within your paper with either in-text parenthetical references (if you are using MLA or APA style) or footnotes (if you are using Chicago style.) If you are unsure which citation style to use, check with the faculty member who is teaching the course.

Below are examples of in-text parenthetical references and footnotes. For more information and examples, see the <u>Citation styles</u> section of this Website.

In-text Parenthetical References (MLA and APA)

With this method, you identify the resource within the text of your paper and then provide an alphabetical list of the resources you used at the end of the paper where the full publishing information is provided. You would use a parenthetical reference any time you <u>quote, paraphrase, or summarize</u>.

MLA

Excerpt from a research paper:

The Ku Klux Klan has a website, as do many other groups who are prejudiced against others - whether on the basis of race, sexual orientation, religion, etc. "The World Wide Web has allowed marginalized extremist groups with messages of hate to have a more visible and accessible public platform" (Leets 287).

OR, with a <u>signal phrase</u>

The Ku Klux Klan has a website, as do many other groups who are prejudiced against others - whether on the basis of race, sexual orientation, religion, etc. According to Leets, "the World Wide Web has allowed marginalized extremist groups with messages of hate to have a more visible and accessible public platform" (287).

MLA citation from Works Cited list:

Leets, Laura. "Responses to Internet Hate Sites: Is Speech Too Free in Cyberspace?" Communication Law & Policy 6.2 (2001): 287. Academic Search Premier. EBSCOhost. Mantor Library, UMF. 24 May 2002 <http://www.epnet.com>.

(This citation does not look exactly as it should in your list of works cited. It should be double spaced with hanging indents. To see proper format of citations, go to Citation styles.)

APA

Excerpt from a research paper:

The Ku Klux Klan has a website, as do many other groups who are prejudiced against others - whether on the basis of race, sexual orientation, religion, etc. "The World Wide Web has allowed marginalized extremist groups with messages of hate to have a more visible and accessible public platform" (Leets, 2001, p. 287).

OR, with a signal phrase

The Ku Klux Klan has a website, as do many other groups who are prejudiced against others - whether on the basis of race, sexual orientation, religion, etc. According to Leets (2001), "the World Wide Web has allowed marginalized extremist groups with messages of hate to have a more visible and accessible public platform" (p. 287).

APA citation from References list:

Leets, L. (2001). Responses to Internet hate sites: Is speech too free in cyberspace? Communication Law & Policy, 6(2), 287. Retrieved May 24, 2002, from Academic Search Premier database.

(This citation does not look exactly as it should in your list of works cited. It should be double spaced with hanging indents. To see proper format of citations, go to Citation styles.)

Footnotes (Chicago)

This method uses superscript (raised) numbers at the end of a quote, paraphrase, or summary to link the reader to the resource which is located at the bottom of the page (footnote.)

Chicago

Excerpt from a research paper:

The Ku Klux Klan has a website, as do many other groups who are prejudiced against others - whether on the basis of race, sexual orientation, religion, etc. "The World Wide Web has allowed marginalized extremist groups with messages of hate to have a more visible and accessible public platform."[1]

Footnote at the bottom of the page:

[1] Laura L. Leets, "Responses to Internet Hate Sites: Is Speech Too Free in Cyberspace?," *Communication Law & Policy* 6, no. 2 (2001): 287. EBSCOhost: Academic Search Premier [database online]. EBSCO Publishing. EBSCO Information Services Group, accessed 24 May 2002.

(The note above does not look exactly as it should in your paper. The first line needs to be indented. If the note falls onto subsequent lines, they should align to the left and be double-spaced.)

Giving Credit - Presentations, Websites, etc.

When you incorporate someone else's work (words, statistics, graphs, charts, images, audio, video, etc.) into a presentation you are preparing or a website you are creating, it is extremely important to give credit where credit is due.

Why? First of all, it is just common courtesy. If you have used someone else's work, the least you can do is offer thanks by acknowledging him/her. In addition to courtesy, giving credit will help you to avoid plagiarizing. **Using someone's else's ideas, words, or other creations without clearly acknowledging where they came from is plagiarism.** (It may also be an infringement of copyright. While plagiarism is unethical, infringing copyright is illegal. For more information on copyright, see the What's the deal with the © ? section of this website.)

To avoid plagiarizing, you must give credit whenever you use any piece of information that is not common knowledge. This includes

- the words, ideas, opinions, or theories of others whether quoted, summarized or paraphrased (For more information, see the Quoting, paraphrasing, and summarizing section of this tutorial.)

- facts, statistics, graphs, charts, images, audio, video, etc. generated/created by someone other than you

When you present information that is not in a paper, it is vital that you relay to your audience where the information came from. Giving credit to your sources can be accomplished through words and/or what you include on PowerPoint slides or other visual aids.

Whether you are presenting information to a classroom of peers or a meeting room of professionals, several situations will arise in which you must credit sources:

Speeches   Presentations   Websites   Articles

Speeches

You are writing a speech on the topic of homelessness and find some great statistics from the Institute for Children on Poverty. Below are two sample passages for your speech that incorporate these statistics. Which one gives credit to the source?

> Last year, 37% of families on welfare had their benefits reduced or terminated. Of those, 20% said that contributed directly to their homelessness.

> A survey of homeless shelters around the US last year by the Institute for Children in Poverty found that 37% of families on welfare had their benefits reduced or terminated. Of those, 20% said that contributed directly to their homelessness.

The second one, right?! This passage will let the audience know exactly where the information came from.

Presentations

You are preparing a PowerPoint presentation on homeschooling. You find some data from the National Center for Education Statistics you want to include. Below are two sample PowerPoint slides. Which one gives credit to the source?

How Many Children are Homeschooled in the US?

According to the *National Center for Education Statistics*:

- 850,000 in Spring 1999 *(= 1.7% of students, ages 5 to 17)*

  o 82% homeschooled only

  o 18% enrolled in public or private schools part time

  o 75% were white, non-Hispanic

How Many Children are Homeschooled in the US?

- 850,000 in Spring 1999 *(= 1.7% of students, ages 5 to 17)*

  o   82% homeschooled only

  o   18% enrolled in public or private schools part time

  o   75% were white, non-hispanic

If you said the first slide, you're right!

Giving credit also applies to images, charts, graphs, audio, video etc., not created by you, that you incorporate into your presentations. Somewhere near the item (above, below, or next to), be sure to indicate the source. For example, you are putting together a PowerPoint presentation on milfoil. You found a great picture of it on the Maine Department of Environmental Protection's website. Here's how you could put it on a PowerPoint slide and give credit.

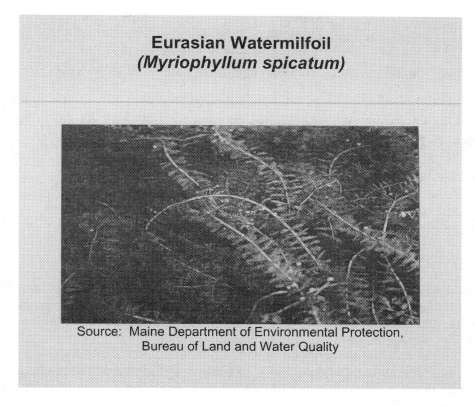

Eurasian Watermilfoil
(Myriophyllum spicatum)

Source: Maine Department of Environmental Protection,
Bureau of Land and Water Quality

Websites

For websites and pages, the form giving credit takes varies.

If your Web page reads like a research paper or documented essay, you should give credit as you would in a typed paper - with either parenthetical in-text references or footnotes. (For more information on how create these, see the Giving Credit - Papers page.) Here are some examples of Web pages that incorporate in-text parenthetical references or footnotes.

Bilingualism and Bilingual Education: A Research Perspective
http://www.ncela.gwu.edu/pubs/focus/focus1.htm

Note the use of in-text parenthetical references and the presence of an alphabetical list of the cited resources at the bottom of the page.

Fatality Facts: Motorcycles
http://www.highwaysafety.org/safety_facts/fatality_facts/motorcyl.htm

Note the use of superscript (raised) numbers throughout the text and a listing of footnotes at the bottom of the page.

Another option for giving credit in web pages is to include the sources of information within the text.

Obesity and Diabetes in Children
http://www.drgreene.com/21_939.html

Note, in the text, the reference to the March 14, 2002 issue of *New England Journal of Medicine*.

If you create and incorporate tables or graphs in your web page, be sure to indicate the source(s) of the data.

Violent Juvenile Crime in California
http://www.hrw.org/prisons/ca/graph1.htm

Note the list of *Sources* below the graph.

Images, Audio, and Video

In a classroom setting, a multimedia presentation you create (with a program like PowerPoint) has a limited audience - the instructor and/or your classmates. Images, graphs/charts, and audio and video clips from other sources may be incorporated provided the sources are cited properly.

When you create a Web page and publish it on the World Wide Web, it immediately becomes available to anyone in the world with Web access. Incorporating images, audio, and/or video not created by you and citing them properly may keep you from plagiarizing, however, this may not prevent you from committing **copyright infringement**. (While plagiarizing is unethical, copyright infringement is illegal. For more information on copyright, see the <u>What's the deal with the © ?</u> section of this website.)

An example - You are taking a nutrition class and, as a project, you are creating a website on veganism. You own a cookbook with vegan recipes and have decided to include some of them in your site. To avoid plagiarism, you cited the sources of the recipes, but have you infringed copyright?

By making recipes freely available on the Web from a cookbook that would have otherwise had to be purchased, you may be in violation of copyright.

Another example - You are taking a geography class, and as a project, you are creating a website on Norway. On the Web, you found a great graphic - an outline of the country with the flag in the middle. You copy this graphic and paste it into your Web page. To avoid plagiarism, you cite the source of the graphic, but have you infringed copyright?

Making a derivative work (a Web page that includes a copy of a copyrighted image), is a violation of copyright. The copyright owner has the exclusive right "to prepare derivative works based upon the copyrighted work." (Title 17, U.S.C., Section 106).

Is it possible to create a Web page that includes images, audio and/or video created by someone other than you and avoid copyright infringement? Of course! Here are three ways.

1. Take steps to ensure your use of an image or audio or video clip falls within the "fair use" guidelines. The fair use provision of the copyright statute allows for the reproduction of parts of copyrighted materials **without** permission of the copyright owner. (See the <u>What is "fair use?"</u> page of this website for more information.)

For example, each spring the <u>Mantor Library</u> organizes a <u>One Book, One Campus</u> program. The website that is put together with information on the program and events always includes a downloaded or scanned image of the cover of the book. This use of a copyrighted image falls under the fair use guidelines.

2. Get permission from the copyright holder to use the image or audio or video clip.

Contact the person or organization that is making the image or audio or video clip available on the Web. Ask for permission to incorporate it into your Web page. In your request, assure the person or organization that if granted permission, you will cite the resource properly and indicate that permission was granted.

3. Link to the image or audio or video clip instead of making it available on your own Web page.

For example, you are taking a music class and creating a Web page on the didgeridoo. You found a great audio clip of someone playing this musical instrument on a Web page. Instead of downloading the file and making it available from your Web page, create a link from your Web page to the Web page with the audio clip.

Articles

Articles written for newspapers, popular magazines, and newsletters do not contain formal citations as research papers or documented essays would. Instead, the author includes sources of information within the text of the article.

Excerpt from a newspaper article

> U.S. Transportation Secretary Norm Mineta said in Minneapolis on Monday he wants to restore people's faith in flying and make air travel convenient, but he said racial profiling is not the answer to ensuring security at the nation's commercial airports.
>
> "People have said, 'Why not racially profile?' Security analysts have told us in-depth, racially profiling by itself is not going to do the job," said Mineta, who was sent to live in an internment camp during World War II because of his Japanese ancestry.
>
> "Racial profiling will not be a method of doing enforcement," he said. Instead, strange behavior will be among the things security screeners look at, he said.
>
> His remarks came during a conference at the University of Minnesota on how transportation should change after Sept. 11.

(Source)

In this example, the author has identified the speaker (Norm Mineta), quoted his remarks, and stated where (University of Minnesota), when (Monday), and in what context (conference on how transportation should change after Sept. 11) the remarks were made.

Excerpt from a newsletter article

> A new national poll from the Children's Institute International (CII) in Los Angeles reveals that a majority of adults believe that children sometimes need a "good, hard spanking." The survey found that 82 percent of adults surveyed were spanked as children and that 55 percent believe spanking is necessary.
>
> "It's worrisome that spanking remains such a part of the American culture, in view of scientific evidence demonstrating its ill effects," says Steve Ambrose, Ph.D., clinical psychologist and director of research at CII. "This suggests the need for continued public education. There is a wealth of research data showing that violent parenting produces violent children; so does negligent parenting. We are not saying parents shouldn't discipline their children, but there are more appropriate and effective ways than hitting them."

(Source)

In this example, the author indicates the source of the statistics (a CII poll) and the name and credentials of the person quoted (Steve Ambrose, Ph.D, clinical psychologist and director of research at CII.)

Citation styles

As you write your paper and prepare your bibliography (a list of the resources you used), remember that every source you use in your paper **MUST** be cited. This includes books, articles, websites, graphics, charts, etc.

If you do not cite your resources, you may be accused of plagiarism. Why else is it important to cite your resources?

- Citations give credit to the authors of the resources you used to write your paper. If you have used someone else's ideas, words, graphics, etc., it is important to give credit where it is due.
- Citations will allow the reader to identify and locate the sources you used. Perhaps a reader will want to read the book or article you cited for more information on the topic.
- Citations lend credibility and authority to your research paper or project.

The links in the table below lead to more information and examples on the most commonly used citation styles at UMF.   If you are not sure which citation style to use for your course, check with the faculty member who is teaching it.

When using	within your paper, you should use	The page at the end that lists all of the resources you used should be titled
MLA, (Modern Language Association)	in-text parenthetical references.	Works Cited.
APA, (American Psychological Association)	in-text parenthetical references.	References.
CBE: Name-Year System (Council of Biology Editors)	in-text parenthetical references.	References.

History Writing Guidelines - The UMF History department offers these guidelines on writing and citation style.

Is it plagiarism? (interactive game)

1. You write a paper on the legalization of marijuana for your high school Current Events class. You save that paper and hand it in to satisfy the persuasive paper requirement in your English Composition 100F class here at UMF. Is it plagiarism?

YES   NO

2. You are working on a computer slide show presentation for your literature class. You want to make the point that Shakespeare's works have been plagiarized throughout the centuries. You capture a painting of Shakespeare from the Web for your first slide. Is it plagiarism?

YES   NO

3. In your computer slide show presentation about Shakespeare's works, you include a snippet of famous dialogue from Romeo and Juliet. Is it plagiarism?

YES   NO

4. You decide the best way to get across your point about Shakespeare's works being plagiarized is to show some examples. You include a video clip from the film West Side Story in your presentation. Is it plagiarism?

YES   NO

5. Your professor says some interesting things in today's lecture on Plato. You decide to use her ideas to begin your paper. Is it plagiarism?

YES   NO

6. Here's an appropriate source for a paper on cyberhate speech.

Rothman, Jeniffer E. "Freedom of Speech and True Threats." Harvard Journal of Law and Public Policy 25.1 (Fall 2001): 85 pp. Academic Search Premier. EBSCOhost. 6410679. Mantor Lib., Farmington, ME. 10 Jun. 2002 <http://ehostvgw3.epnet.com>.

(This citation does not look exactly as it should in your list of works cited. It should be double spaced with hanging indents. To see proper format of citations, go to Citation styles.)

Rothman addresses the growth of Internet hate speech:

"The law surrounding threats has gained recent attention from commentators after decades of virtual anonymity and unaddressed confusion among the lower courts. The sudden interest in threats has been sparked primarily by the proliferation of widely disseminated Internet speech[5]" (Rothman 286).

You decide to use this quote as-is. Is it plagiarism?

YES   NO

7. You decide to use this passage from the introductory section of the Rothman article:

You are a physician at a local Planned Parenthood clinic. As part of your job you perform abortions. There have been protests outside the clinic and you have heard about the murders of several doctors around the country who were killed because they performed abortions. One day a colleague calls you and tells you that an anti-abortion group has put up a website which lists the names and home addresses of doctors who perform abortions. When you look at the website you find your name and address on the list along with strong language accountable for your crimes against humanity. Some of the doctors' names have black lines through them. You recognize these names as people who have been murdered by anti-abortion fanatics. Can you successfully sue the creators of the website for threatening you and causing you severe emotional distress, or is this website protected by the First Amendment?[1] Now imagine yourself a woman in college. You hear from a friend that a classmate has posted a story about you on the Internet with a newsgroup called "sex stories." You read the posting and find a gruesome and detailed story of the narrator torturing and raping you. The story culminates in a description of you being doused with kerosene and lit on fire. The posting uses your real name. You are scared and call the police. Should your classmate be convicted of threatening you?[2] You attend a rally in support of a boycott of white-owned stores whose owners will not hire African American employees. You are aware of several violent acts against blacks who have ignored the boycott including the firing of shots into the house of one boycott violator. The leader of the boycott speaks at the rally and warns boycott violators that "their necks will be broken." You had been considering returning to some of the white-own stores but are frightened by the leader's words. Should the leader of the boycott be arrested for threatening boycott violators or is his speech protected by the First Amendment?[3] (Rothman 284-285)

Is it plagiarism?

<u>YES</u>   <u>NO</u>

8. You read this passage in the Rothman article:

This article proposes a new test for determining what is a true threat. The reasonable speaker/listener test, adopted by a majority of circuits, is useful but incomplete. I add two additional elements to my test: (1) a subjective intent prong which requires the prosecution or plaintiff to prove that the speaker purposely, knowingly, or recklessly intimidated, frightened, or coerced the target; and (2) an actor prong which requires proof that the speaker explicitly or implicitly suggest that he or his co-conspirators will be the ones to carry out the threat. In addition, I develop in more detail the factors that a fact-finder should consider when applying the reasonable listener prong.   The addition of the actor prong is wholly novel and has not been discussed by courts or scholars to date.[18] This prong is crucial to my test, and crucial to the protection of speech under any test for determining whether a true threat has been made. By requiring that there be, at the very least, some implication that the speaker or his associates will be the ones to carry out the threat, greater latitude is given to speakers to use, without fear of punishment, the strong language that the First Amendment allows. (Rothman 289)

You decide to use this concept in your paper. You write the following:

Instead of relying on the reaction of the victim, why not look at the intent of the perpetrator? If the speaker clearly intended to intimidate the victim, suggesting that the speaker him/herself or his/her cronies will commit violence against the victim, then the speech is not protected.

Is it plagiarism?

<u>YES</u>   <u>NO</u>

9. You use the same passage in a different way.

This article proposes a new test for determining what is a true threat. The reasonable speaker/listener test, adopted by a majority of circuits, is useful but incomplete. I add two additional elements to my test: (1) a subjective intent prong which requires the prosecution or plaintiff to prove that the speaker purposely, knowingly, or recklessly intimidated, frightened, or coerced the target; and (2) an actor prong which requires proof that the speaker explicitly or implicitly suggest that he or his co-conspirators will be the ones to carry out the threat. In addition, I develop in more detail the factors that a fact-finder should consider when applying the reasonable listener prong.   The addition of the actor prong is wholly novel and has not been discussed by   courts or scholars to date. This prong is crucial to my test, and crucial to the protection of speech under any test for determining whether a true threat has been made. By requiring that there be, at the very least, some implication that the speaker or his associates will be the ones to carry out the threat, greater latitude is given to speakers to use, without fear of punishment, the strong language that the First Amendment allows. (Rothman 289)

You decide to paraphrase the first part, eliminating the need to indent a long block quote.

Rothman proposes a new test for deciding what is a true threat. The reasonable speaker/listener test used in many circuit courts, is a good starting place, but is not enough. He adds two additional elements to the test: (1) an intent prong that requires that the prosecution prove that the speaker meant to intimidate, frighten, or coerce the victim; and (2) an actor prong that requires proof that the accused speaker made it clear that he was suggesting that he or his co-conspirators would carry out the threat (289).

Is it plagiarism?

YES   NO

Use valid, credible sources for information

Just because you have located a book, article, website, or other resource on your topic, does not mean you should automatically use it in your paper or project. You need to choose your resources carefully to make sure you get the best and most useful ones.

How can you tell if the book, article, website, or other resource you located is a valid, credible source? It may be helpful for you to ask yourself six questions:

Who?	Who is the author? What are his/her credentials?
What?	What information is available from this resource?
Where?	Where did the author(s) get the information? Are citations provided?
When?	When was the resource produced? (For books, check the copyright date. For articles, check the publication date. For websites, look for a "created on" or "last updated on" date.)
Why?	Why does this resource exist? Is the purpose to

entertain, persuade, inform, etc.? Is the resource biased?

How? How comprehensive is the resource? Does it go into the depth you need?

Take careful notes

Copying and pasting is not necessarily plagiarism. Look at it this way: What did people do to write research papers before the Internet and cheap photocopies? They went to the library with a stack of note cards and wrote down summaries, quotes, and paraphrases, carefully noting the page number of each piece of information. You can do the same basic thing with your computer. Think of the process as creating electronic note cards.

Step 1. Prewrite and research.

Let's pretend you're writing the paper in MLA style for your English Composition 100F class. The broad topic is the First Amendment. Using the brainstorming method, you narrow the topic to freedom of speech, narrow it again to hate speech, and go looking for sources. After a quick search on one of the library's databases, you find you can narrow the topic even further to Internet hate speech, or cyberhate. Gather your sources and record all the bibliographic information. To save time, have your citation style handbook (MLA, APA, Chicago, CBE) handy (or go to the citation styles section of this website) and type in the information in the required format. That way, there's little chance you will leave out a required piece of information. And if you have a full citation, you'll be able to find the source again in no time.

Here's a source that would be valuable for your cyberhate paper.

Leets, Laura. "Responses to Internet Hate Sites: Is Speech Too Free in Cyberspace?." Communication Law and Policy 6.2 (Fall 2001): 31 pp. Academic Search Premier. EBSCOhost. 4792666. Mantor Lib., Farmington, ME. 10 Jun. 2002 <http://ehostvgw3.epnet.com> .

(You found the source on a database, so the citation must show the path you took to find the article. This citation does not look exactly as it should in your list of works cited. It should be double spaced with hanging indents. To see proper format of citations, go to Citation styles.)

See this citation in APA style or Chicago style.

Go to Step 2: Choose a passage from the source

Quoting, paraphrasing, and summarizing

In the Take careful notes section, you learned how to generate electronic note cards by copying and pasting information in a way that does not invite plagiarism. Once you have the information at hand, you must decide how it will best fit into your paper: as a quote, a paraphrase, or a summary. Before making that decision, here are some things to consider:

- Do not make the mistake of reading all your sources without taking notes and then trying to go back and find the information you remember. You must show where you got your information.

- Break up the information so that you have only one idea per note.

- Always place quotation marks around the notes you copy and paste; the computer does not know you are copying a direct quote unless you tell it.

- Use a quote in your final draft when the author's words are the best way to express the information.

- Be wary of long quotes. Too many long quotes will make your paper more someone else's words than your own plagiarism.

- Paraphrase carefully, never echoing the sentence structure used in the original text.

- Summarize by shortening the information to a manageable length. A summary should be much shorter than what's being summarized.

See how to incorporate information by

quoting.

paraphrasing.

summarizing.

What happens if you are accused?

If you are worried about being accused of plagiarism, your best defense is to do your own work, keep careful track of your sources and notes, understand everything you have written, and acknowledge those who contribute to your work. **Giving credit to sources is not an afterthought; it is at the core of academic life.**

The University of Maine at Farmington Code of Academic Integrity spells out the sanctions that may be imposed on those who are accused of an an academic integrity violation.

The Code of Academic Integrity also lays out the procedures faculty members must follow to make an accusation of violation of the code. The Academic Integrity Violation Form allows students to respond to an accusation.

WELCOME STUDENTS
TO
"ACADEMIC INTEGRITY"

General Integrity Information

Academic Integrity Guides, Resources, and Tips

Helping Students to Avoid Plagiarism

Plagiarism Detection and links to Articles about Plagiarism

Student Academic Policy

Violations of Student Academic Integrity

Sanctions for Student Violations of Academic Integrity

Procedures for Student Violations of Academic Integrity

Hearing of Student Violations of Academic Integrity

Appeal of the Findings of the Student Academic Integrity Board

Student Rights in Alleged Violations of Student Academic Integrity

Faculty Rights in Alleged Violations of Student Academic Integrity

****

General Integrity Information

Why Integrity Matters: This site offers a good discussion of the importance and relationship of personal integrity and the future of American society.
http://sja.ucdavis.edu/integ1.htm

Center for Academic Integrity web site. Links to other University honor codes as well resource links to information on academic integrity, ethics, and values.
http://www.academicintegrity.org/

Academic Integrity Guides, Resources, and Tips

Purdue University: "Academic Integrity: A Guide for Students."
http://www.purdue.edu/odos/administration/integrity.htm.

University of Florida: "Academic Honesty-Student Guide."
http://dso.ufl.edu/judicial/academicguide.htm.

 This site has several examples of academic dishonesty.
http://www.queensu.ca/secretariat/senate/policies/acaddish.html

This site has some basic types of academic dishonesty behaviors that are unacceptable.
http://www.northwestern.edu/uacc/defines.html

This page has some examples on 'acceptable borrowing'.
http://osu.orst.edu/admin/stucon/plag.htm

This site has a nice list of bookmarks that give different examples of academic dishonesty and also good examples for citations.
http://www.law.gwu.edu/resources/citing.asp

Helping Students to Avoid Plagiarism

This site offers a comprehensive guide for conducting research, proper citations (APA, MLA and electronic) and writing papers.
http://owl.english.purdue.edu/handouts/research/index.html

Plagiarism: What It Is and How to Recognize and Avoid It (Indiana University Bloomington)
http://www.indiana.edu/~wts/wts/plagiarism.html

Plagiary and the Art of Skillful Citation
http://www.bcm.tmc.edu/immuno/citewell

Plagiarism Detection and links to Articles about Plagiarism

Turnitin.com
http://www.turnitin.com

Glatt Plagiarism Services
http://www.plagiarism.com/

STUDENT ACADEMIC INTEGRITY POLICY

The academic community of the University of Southern Maine recognizes that adherence to high principles of academic integrity is vital to the academic function of the University.

Academic integrity is based upon honesty. All students of the University are expected to be honest in their academic endeavors. All academic work should be performed in a manner which will provide an honest reflection of the knowledge and abilities of each student. Any breach of academic honesty should be regarded as a serious offense by all members of the academic community.

The entire academic community shares the responsibility for establishing and maintaining standards of academic integrity. Those in charge of academic tasks have an obligation to make known the standards and expectations of acceptable academic conduct. Each student has an obligation to know and understand those standards and expectations. While the academic community recognizes that the responsibility for learning and personal conduct is an individual matter, all students and faculty members are expected to help to maintain academic integrity at the University by refusing to participate in, or tolerate, any dishonesty.

We recognize that there is an educational component to the student academic integrity policy and its associated behaviors at the university. This policy must be linked to efforts to educate students, faculty and staff regarding definitions, concepts and issues associated with academic integrity.

Violations of Student Academic Integrity

Academic integrity means not lying, cheating, or stealing. To cheat on an examination, to steal the words or ideas of another, or to falsify the results of one's research corrupts the essential process by which knowledge is advanced. Cheating, plagiarism, fabrication of data, giving or receiving unauthorized help on examinations, and other acts of academic dishonesty are contrary to the academic purposes for which the University exists.

Violations of student academic integrity include any actions which attempt to promote or enhance the academic standing of any student by dishonest means. The following is a listing of some, but not necessarily all, actions that are violations of academic integrity:

1. Cheating on an academic exercise. Cheating includes giving or receiving unauthorized aid or information by copying, by using materials not authorized, by attempting to receive credit for work performed by another, or by otherwise failing to abide by academic rules. The person who aids an individual in cheating holds equal responsibility for the cheating.

2. Plagiarizing the words, ideas, or data of others by not giving proper acknowledgement of sources. Plagiarism includes failing to identify verbatim statements as quotations and failing to give appropriate credit and citations of sources used.

Study, preparation, and presentation should involve at all times the student's own work as much as possible. It is a proper part of the learning process to incorporate the thoughts or ideas of others into one's own mind and one's own presentations with the purpose of learning and enlarging personal boundaries of knowledge. When a new idea is learned from the work of others, however, there is a clear distinction between the presentation of that idea with acknowledgement of sources and the presentation of the idea as one's own. Any work that the student borrows from others must be suitably identified with appropriate citations because conscientious acknowledgement of sources is always required by the principles of academic integrity.

It is understood by the academic community that the principles of academic integrity require that all work submitted or presented without citation of sources will be the student's own work, not only on tests, but in themes, papers, homework, and class presentations, unless it has been clearly specified that the work is a team effort.

3. Fabricating information with intent to deceive. Fabrication includes, but is not limited to, falsifying experimental data or results, inventing research or laboratory data or results for work not done, knowingly presenting falsified or invented results, citing information not taken from the source indicated, falsely claiming sources not used, and that are known to be false, misleading, or not supported by evidence.

Conclusions or opinions that are presented must be drawn from genuine research or data or from well known information unless they are clearly identified as being speculation or supposition.

4. Submitting any academic accomplishment in whole or in part for credit more than once whether in the same course or in different courses without the prior consent of the instructors.

5. Obtaining or attempting to obtain an examination, or any part of it, before the examination has been given.

6. Obtaining or attempting to obtain an examination. Or any part of it, after the examination has been given when specifically prohibited.

7. Intentionally attempting to interfere with or prevent others from having fair and equal access to the resources of the University's libraries or the University's computers including the intentional damaging or destroying of any materials or computer files.

8. Copying, editing, or deleting computer files without permission.

9. Altering, changing, or forging University academic records or forging the signature of any academic officer.

Sanctions for Student Violations of Academic Integrity

A student who admits to being guilty or who is found to be guilty of a violation of academic integrity will be subject to appropriate sanctions. Sanctions will be determined in accordance with the Procedures for Student Violations of Academic Integrity. The exact penalty will depend upon the particular circumstances of each individual case. Graduate students will, in general, be held to a higher standard.

Student violations of academic integrity may be either course related or non-course related. A course-related violation of academic integrity is any offense that may be committed for the purpose of promoting or enhancing the academic standing of the student who commits the offense. A non-course related violation of academic integrity is any offense that does not affect the academic standing of the person committing the offense.

The following is a list of possible sanctions that may be imposed upon students for multiple, course-related, violations of academic integrity or for any number of non-course-related violations of academic integrity. This list shall not be taken to be exhaustive and may be modified or enlarged to meet particular circumstances in any given situation. A combination of two or more of these sanctions may be imposed when justified by the type of violation.

1. Dismissal from the University. Severance of the student's relationship with the University of Maine System. Readmission is possible

only in accordance with the review process outlined in the UMS Student Conduct Code.

2. Suspension from the University for a stated period of time up to one academic year during which time the student will not be allowed to take any courses in the University of Maine System. The University of Southern Maine will not accept nor give credit for any courses taken at another institution during suspension.

3. Probation. Notification that further violations of academic integrity will result in suspension or dismissal from the University, depending on the seriousness of the violation. The period of probation to be specified for the particular situation; normally for no more than one academic year. Probation may include loss of one or more privileges such as representing the University in an intercollegiate event or contest, participation in extracurricular activities, or appointment to any University committee.

4. Appropriate grade penalties up to and including F grades in one or more involved courses. For a single, first-time, course-related violation of academic integrity, the maximum penalty impose will not be greater than a grade of F for the course. Course instructors may exercise discretion in prescribing lesser penalties or additional academic tasks appropriate to allow the student to complete a course and thereby receive a grade representing demonstrated knowledge of the course.

5. Loss of some or all of the benefits of programs, scholarships, and other opportunities normally afforded students as support and recognition for superior academic achievement. This would not include any need-based federal financial aid programs.

6. Academic conduct probation for a stated period of time, normally for no more than one academic year, during which time any further violation of academic integrity will constitute grounds for more severe sanctions.

7. Restitution for damages done to any library materials or computer files. (Damaging library materials or computer files may also subject the student to civil or criminal penalties.)

8. Completion of an assignment to work a specific number of hours at a designated community service activity.

9. Such other action as may be appropriate.

Procedures for Student Violations of Academic Integrity

A. Charges of Student Violations of Academic Integrity.

When, in the opinion of a faculty member, an administrative officer, or a student, a violation of student academic integrity has occurred, these procedures shall be followed in a reasonable and timely fashion:

Charge by a Faculty Member:

1. The faculty member will inform the student in private of the specific charge and the aspect of academic integrity that is alleged to have been violated. The student may explain the circumstances and attempt to justify the action if the student chooses. The charge may be dropped if an explanation by the student is accepted as being adequate.

2. If the faculty member chooses to continue the complaint, with or without an explanation by the student, the faculty member will verify through the Office of Community Standards whether or not the violation is a first offense.

3. If the faculty member confirms that a course-related violation of academic integrity is a first offense, the faculty member may choose to deal with the offense without further consulting the Office of Community Standards. In this case, regardless of whether or not the student has responded to the changes, the faculty member will impose a penalty up to and including a grade of F in the course. If the proposed sanction is approved by the chair of the department, program or school in which the course is taught (and/or the next higher academic officer if the chair is unavailable or is the person bringing the sanction) the faculty member will notify the student in writing of the charge and the sanction imposed.

The letter from the faculty member to the student will include a notice that the student has the right to contest the action by appealing to the Office of Community Standards in writing within seven calendar days of receiving the letter of notification.

4. The faculty member will send a copy of the charge letter to the Office of Community Standards for placement in the student's file. NOTE: Given that the student has the right to appeal the faculty member's decision, no action on the sanctions imposed will be taken until after it has been verified that the student did not appeal.

5. If the student wishes to contest the charge or the sanction imposed by the faculty member, the student will have seven calendar days from receipt of the letter of notification to present a letter of appeal to the Office of Community Standards. The Student Conduct Officer will initiate the appeal process and the Chair of the Student Academic Integrity Board will convene the Student Academic Integrity Board as soon as is feasible.

6. If the faculty member finds that there is evidence of multiple or repeated violations of academic integrity by the student, the complaint will be referred to the Office of Community Standards for appropriate action. In this case, the faculty member will not take any punitive action against the student. Any sanctions to be imposed will be determined by the Student Academic Integrity Board through procedures of fundamental fairness.-

Charge by an Administrative Officer:

The administrative officer will notify the Office of Community Standards of the specific charge in writing. The Student Conduct Officer will initiate the hearing process and the Chair of the Student Academic Integrity Board will convene the Student Academic Integrity Board as soon as is feasible. A student will not be required to withdraw from courses or from the University before the hearing process is completed.

Charge by a Student:

The student making the charge will notify the Office of Community Standards of the specific charge in writing. The Student Conduct Officer will initiate the hearing process and the and the Chair of the Student Academic Integrity Board will convene the Student Academic Integrity Board as soon as is feasible. A student will not be required to withdraw from courses or from the University before the hearing process is completed.

B. Hearing of Student Violations of Academic Integrity.

Any hearing related to violations of student academic integrity will be conducted the Student Academic Integrity Board in accordance with the following guidelines:

1. The Chair of the Student Academic Integrity Board shall make every reasonable effort to insure that the Board hears each case promptly at a time that is convenient for all concerned.

2. Arrangements shall be made for keeping an audio tape record of the proceedings of the hearing.

   a. In cases of appeal, the student charged with the violation, and authorized University officials may have access to the tapes for the purpose of review relating to the appeal.

   b. Such tapes shall be kept by the University for seven years after all appeal rights have been exhausted; The tapes shall then be destroyed.

   c. Audio-taped records of hearings are deemed to be Student Education Records under the Family Education Rights and Privacy Act of 1974 and may not be disclosed publicly without the consent of the student charged with the violation and all other students named on the tape or as provided in that Act.

3. The student who has been charged with a violation of academic integrity and the person who has made the charge should both be present at the hearing.

   a. If the student charged with a violation or the person who has made the charge is not present at the time appointed for the hearing, the Chair of the Student Academic Integrity Board shall first attempt to determine the reason for that person's absence. The Board may then proceed in a normal manner, may hear any appropriate portion of the testimony and adjourn to a later date, or may continue the entire hearing to a later date. The Board may not consider the absence of any party as relevant to whether or not the accused student committed the alleged violation of academic integrity.

   b. The student charged with a violation, the Student Conduct Officer, and the person who has made the charge shall each have the right to challenge for cause any member of the Board by submitting to the Chair of the Student Academic Integrity Board a written statement of the grounds for this challenge at least two days prior to the scheduled hearing. Removal of members of the Board for cause shall be within the authority of and at the discretion of the Chair of the Board or the Vice-Chair of the Board if the Chair is not able to exercise that function or if the Chair has been challenged for cause.

4. The student charged has the right to have up to two support people at the hearing. The hearing shall normally be open, but it must be closed at the request of the student who has been charged with a violation of academic integrity or at the request of the person who has made the charge. The Chair of the Student Academic Integrity Board may close the hearing or a portion of the hearing to protect witnesses or other parties. If the hearing is closed, the Chair shall stress the confidentiality of the hearing.

5. At the beginning of the hearing:
   a. The Chair of the Student Academic Integrity Board shall:

      1. Outline and review the procedures to be followed throughout the hearing process
      2. Review the charges.

   b. The person who had made the charge shall summarize the evidence that constitutes the basis for the charge. If the person who had made the charge is not present, the Student Conduct Officer or the Chair of the Student Academic Integrity Board shall summarize the evidence that constitutes the basis for the charge.

   c. The student who has been charged with a violation of academic integrity may contest the charges by presenting an explanation or other appropriate evidence to justify reduction or dismissal of the charges.

6. During the presentation of evidence:

   a. The student who has been charged with a violation of academic integrity and the person who had made the charge may both call witnesses and present additional evidence if they wish to do so.-

   b. All parties may be accompanied by an advisor or support person, for example, his/her parent(s), legal guardian(s), or member of the University community. Any party to the proceedings may have legal counsel present to give advice.

   c. Members of the Student Academic Integrity Board may question witnesses or parties to the proceeding.

    d. Witnesses or parties to the proceeding may ask questions of other witnesses or parties to the proceeding only through the Chair of the Student Academic Integrity Board and only at the discretion of the Chair of the Student Conduct Committee.

    e. Cross-examination of any party by any advisor will not be permitted. The advisor will not be permitted to speak at the hearing at such time as his/her advisee's presentation is made to the Committee.

    f. The Chair reserves the right to remove any party from the hearing in order to protect any party participating.

7. After the presentation of all evidence at the hearing:

Each party or their respective advisor(s) may present arguments on the applicability of this Student Academic Integrity Policy or interpretations of any sections within this policy and/or the appropriate sanctions to be assessed if a violation of student academic integrity is found to have been committed.

8. The standard of review to be followed in all proceedings related to student violations of academic integrity shall be fundamental fairness. The standard of proof to be followed in all proceedings related to student violations of academic integrity shall be preponderance of evidence. Strict rules of evidence and procedures will not be required so long as the proceedings are conducted in a manner, which follows fair and full explanations of the circumstances, by both sides. Decisions regarding the admissibility of evidence and the weight to be given to evidence shall be made by the person conducting the hearing in consultation with the members of the Student Academic Integrity Board.

9. The decision of the Student Academic Integrity Board will be based solely upon the evidence presented at the hearing. When determining sanctions to be imposed, the Board will give due consideration to recommendations made both by those who have brought charges and by the student who has been charged with a violation of academic integrity.

10. When a decision has been reached by the Student Academic Integrity Board:

    a. The Chair of the Student Academic Integrity Board shall provide written notice as soon as is practicable to inform the student who has been charged with a violation of academic integrity of the disposition of the case.

    b. The written notice to the student shall include:

        1. The charges found to be true.

        2. A statement that identifies the applicable sections of this Student Academic Integrity Policy that have been violated.

        3. The disciplinary penalties to be imposed on the student.

        4. A statement of the right of the student to appeal the decision of the Board and a statement of the rules governing such an appeal including a statement of the time limit for the filing of an appeal.

    c. Any disciplinary sanctions imposed by the Board shall be effective immediately upon notification unless otherwise specified or unless the student appeals under Section C below in which case sanctions will be stayed unless deemed necessary for the protection of other persons.

11. If the student does not appeal a decision of the Student Academic Integrity Board within the specified time, the decision stands and copies of the written notification will be placed in the student's file in the Office of Community Standards and will be sent to the dean of the school in which the student is registered.

C. Appeal of the Findings of the Student Academic Integrity Board.

Any student who has been found by the Student Academic Integrity Board to violate the principles of academic integrity shall have the right to appeal to the President of the University or to the President's designee for a review of any decision of the Board.

1. The appeal shall be limited to a review of procedures followed and the appropriateness of any sanctions imposed.

2. An appeal shall not result in the imposition of more severe sanctions.

3. The appeal must be in writing and must satisfy the following requirements:

   a. Clearly state the specific charge, recommendation, action, or sanction to which the appeal is related.

   b. Clearly state what procedures or sanctions are appealed.

   c. Present specific reasons, grounds, explanation, or justification to support the appeal.

   d. Be signed by the student making the appeal.

   e. Be submitted within seven calendar days of receipt by the student of notification of the charges or the sanctions that are being appealed.

4. The decision of the President of the University or the President's designee shall be final.

Student Records:

Any sanction for violation of academic integrity will be noted in the student's file in the Office of Community Standards.

The Office of Community Standards serves as the repository of all records of violations of student academic integrity. Such records are normally destroyed seven years after the year the record was created except records pertaining to cases resulting in dismissal, which are held indefinitely.

NOTE: While Lewiston-Auburn College shall establish a Student Academic Integrity Board with jurisdiction over students enrolled in Lewiston-Auburn College degree programs or in USM courses offered at

Lewiston-Auburn College, the Office of Community Standards shall serve as repository for all records.

Membership:

The membership for each Student Academic Integrity Board shall consist of:

> Two (2) full-time faculty members, drawn from the pool of faculty members appointed by the chief academic officer of the university. If the chair is unavailable or unable to serve on the Board the vice-chair serves along with another faculty member.

> Five (5) student members to be drawn from the Student Conduct Committee by the Student Conduct Officer.

The membership of the Student Academic Integrity Board of Lewiston-Auburn College shall consist of:

> Two (2) full-time faculty members, drawn from the pool of faculty members appointed by the chief academic officer of the college. If the chair is unavailable or unable to serve on the Board the vice-chair serves along with another faculty member.

> Five (5) USM student members, three (3) to be appointed by the chief academic officer of the college, and two (2) to be appointed by Student Government.

Terms of Appointment to the Board:

The terms of appointment to the Student Academic Integrity Board for faculty members will be a renewable two (2) years.

Student members will be eligible to serve on the Student Academic Integrity Board for the duration of their appointments to the Student Conduct Committee. The Student Conduct Officer as needed and as available will draw student members from the Student Conduct Committee when a hearing is scheduled. In cases where a graduate student is facing charges, at least two of the students serving on the Board will be graduate students.

The terms of appointment for student members of the Student Academic Integrity Board of Lewiston-Auburn College shall be for 1 or 2 years. These terms are renewable once. No student may serve for more than four years.

Chair:

The Chair and Vice-Chair of the Student Academic Integrity Board (and for Lewiston-Auburn) shall be appointed by the President of the University of Southern Maine. In the absence of the Chair, the Vice Chair shall temporarily perform all the duties of the Chair.

In addition to chairing all hearings, the Chair of the Student Academic Integrity Board, with the assistance of the Student Conduct Officer, shall have the responsibility for scheduling meetings of the Board, notifying parties and witnesses, and reporting the outcome of hearings to the student who has been charged with a violation of academic integrity, the Office of Community Standards, and the person who has made a charge.

Quorum:

A quorum of the Student Academic Integrity Board shall consist of one faculty member (Chair or Vice-Chair) and three students.

Decisions:

All decisions of the Student Academic Integrity Board shall be by a majority vote with at least the above quorum of members present and voting.

The student who has been charged with a violation of academic integrity may appeal decisions of the Student Academic Integrity Board.

Decisions of the Student Academic Integrity Board of Lewiston-Auburn College shall be by a majority vote with at least the above quorum of members present and voting.

Report:

The Student Academic Integrity Board shall prepare an annual report regarding the nature and outcome of the cases heard. This report will be available on request.

<u>Student Rights in Alleged Violations of Student Academic Integrity</u>

Students alleged to have committed a violation of academic integrity shall have the following rights relative to any hearing on the allegations:

1. Written notice shall be provided to the student prior to any hearing. The written notice shall include:
   a. All charges and the complaints upon which the charges are based.
   b. The dates of the alleged occurrences.
   c. The sections of this Student Academic Integrity Policy, which are alleged to have been violated.
   d. The possible sanctions including the maximum sanction that may be imposed if the charges are found to be true.
   e. The time and place at which the hearing will be held.
   f. A statement of the right of the student to appeal.
2. The written notice shall be delivered to the student sufficiently in advance of the hearing provide a reasonable time for the student to prepare a response.
3. The right to reasonable access to the case file. Photocopies of all appropriate materials shall be made available at no expense to the student at the time of the hearing. Prior to the hearing the student is permitted to review all materials in the Office of Community Standards.
4. The right to review all evidence.
5. The right to present evidence and witnesses.
6. The right to have an observer or advisor present during any hearing in accordance with the applicable paragraphs of this Student Academic Integrity Policy contained in section B above entitled "Hearing of Student Violations of Academic Integrity".

Faculty Rights in Alleged Violations of Student Academic Integrity

Members of the faculty have the right to establish appropriate standards of academic performance and expectations for students under their instruction and to assign grades accordingly.

The instructor in charge of an academic course in which an alleged violation of student academic integrity has occurred has the right to be informed of the procedures of the Student Academic Integrity Board and has the right to be present throughout any hearings.

The instructor in charge or an academic course in which an alleged violation of student academic integrity has occurred has the right to be informed of the decision of the Student Academic Integrity Board and the results of appeals.

Except as noted above with respect to jurisdiction and membership for Lewiston-Auburn College, all provisions for the Student Academic Integrity Board shall apply to all cases from the Portland and Gorham campuses and Lewiston-Auburn College.

The authors of this document on student academic integrity gratefully acknowledge that they have freely borrowed, adapted, modified, and used words, phrases, ideas, and concepts found in similar publications of the following educational institutions, listed in alphabetical order:

> Auburn University
>
> Clemson University
>
> University of Delaware
>
> University of Georgia
>
> University of Maine System
>
> Norwich University
>
> University of Tennessee – Knoxville
>
> Texas A & M
>
> Vermont College

University of Wyoming

The policy was approved by President Richard Pattenaude on 2/22/95.

Revisions were approved by the Faculty Senate, March 7, 2003.

This policy was originally published and designed by Student Judicial Affairs September 1995.

Revisions were drafted by Stephen Nelson, Assistant to the Vice President for Community Standards and Jan Burson, Chair, Student Academic Integrity Board. The revised document was presented to the Faculty Senate by the Faculty Senate Academic Standards and Policies Committee.

Contents

This guide provides sources of information on dealing with plagiarism in academic work. The LLC Library Instruction program offers assistance in incorporating information about plagiarism, correct resource citation, and other information literacy topics into course work at UW-Stout.

- Library Instruction

UNIVERSITY OF WISCONSIN-STOUT POLICY

- Student Academic Misconduct/Disciplinary Procedures, Wisconsin Administrative Code, Chapter 14
- UW-Stout Academic Dishonesty Defined
- UW-Stout Student Services statement on Academic Expectations

ACADEMIC AND PROFESSIONAL POLICIES AND ASSISTANCE

- Center for Academic Integrity Includes sample university honor codes and a database of articles on plagiarism.
- JISC Plagiarism Advisory Service Provides advice and tools to institutions, faculty and students.
- Plagiarism Blog Current articles and news about plagiarism
- Defining and Avoiding Plagiarism: The WPA Statement on Best Practices From the Council of Writing Program Administrators

Print Sources in the Library Learning Center

- *Columbia Guide to Online Style* **REF PN171.F56 W35**
- *MLA Handbook for Writers of Research Papers* **REF LB2369 .G53**
- *Plagiarism Handbook: Strategies for Preventing, Detecting, and Dealing With Plagiarism* **PN167 .H37x**
- *Publication Manual of the American Psychological Association* **REF BF76.7 .P83**

CONSTRUCTING ASSIGNMENTS TO DISCOURAGE PLAGIARISM

- Anti-Plagiarism Strategies for Research Papers Article by Robert Harris in online journal *Virtual Salt*
- Discouraging Plagiarism Indiana University Campus Writing Program, Faculty Services
- The New Plagiarism: Seven Antidotes to Prevent Highway Robbery in an Electronic Age Article by Jamie McKenzie in online journal *From Now On, The Educational Technology Journal*
- Search Google using the words *term paper alternatives* for many creative ideas.

SEARCHING FOR THE SOURCE

Use LLC resources to search phrases from the text of papers when plagiarism is suspected.

- Check the works cited and locate the full text in periodical articles in LLC Indexes and Databases. Stout Users Only!
- To find out which full text database includes a particular periodical title, check for the title on the Periodicals Holdings list.
- Check books cited in the paper by searching the Stout Library Catalog and locating the book in the library collection.
- Check for plagiarism from the web by using an "exact phrase" search in the Advanced Search feature of Google or other search engines. Be sure to request results from the full text of the document, not just the title or abstract.

- Search multiple search engines simultaneously using a metasearch engine such as Dogpile.
- Use theTelus Learning Connection Plagiarism Sleuth Tool to search the same exact phrase in several search engines sequentially.

ONLINE PLAGIARISM DETECTION SERVICES

- Copyscape.com Allows web authors to enter urls for their pages and the software checks to see if the content has been used by others.
- EVE2 (Essay Verification Engine) For purchase software that checks essays against the web
- MyDropBox Subscription service that checks text against an internal database as well as the web and produces "originality reports"

- Plagiarism-Finder A commercial program from MediaPhor that searches the web for matches to content in papers on the user's computer
- Plagiarism Resource Site Free plagiarism detection software created by a physics professor from the University of Virginia
- Turnitin.com Subscription software that institutions or individuals can use to check papers against a database of term papers.

AVOIDING PLAGIARISM

- Avoiding Plagiarism University of California-Davis Student Judicial Affairs
- How Not to Plagiarize University of Toronto guide
- Plagiarism An annotated webliography of links to case studies, detection tools, term paper sites
- Purdue University Writing Lab Good hints for keeping track of quotes and citing correctly
- Quoting and Paraphrasing Sources From the UW-Madison Writing Center. Provides good examples of legimate paraphrases vs plagiarized paraphrases.
- Using Sources Hamilton College Writing Center guidelines

A SAMPLING OF TERM PAPER MILLS

- CheatHouse
- Genie 4 Custom Term Papers
- OPPapers.com (Other Peoples' Papers)
- Term Paper Relief Promises "non-plagiarized" custom papers
- Yahoo Research and Term Papers Lists dozens of sites

WWW Search Engines

The search engines that are available on the WWW vary in depth and coverage. Explore the search options to find relevant WWW sites. For a list of available search engines and WWW directories, e.g. Google or Yahoo, use Searching the Web from the Library Home Page.

Citations

To cite online resources in appropriate bibliographic style see: Citing Resources

To organize citations and create bibliographies and papers in APA, MLA and other styles see: RefWorks and Other Citation Management Tools

UWS 14.01 Statement of Principles.

The board of regents, administrators, faculty, academic staff and students of the University of Wisconsin system believe that academic honesty and integrity are fundamental to the mission of higher education and of the University of Wisconsin system. The University has a responsibility to promote academic honesty and integrity and to develop procedures to deal effectively with instances of academic dishonesty. Students are responsible for the honest completion and representation of their work, for the appropriate citation of sources, and for respect of others' academic endeavors. Students who violate these standards must be confronted and must accept the consequences of their actions.

Definitions

UWS 14.03 defines academic misconduct as follows:
- Academic Misconduct Subject to Disciplinary Action
    - Academic misconduct is an act in which a student:
        1. Seeks to claim credit for the work or efforts of another without authorization or citation;
        2. Uses unauthorized materials or fabricated data in any academic exercise;
        3. Forges or falsifies academic documents or records;
        4. Intentionally impedes or damages the academic work of others;
        5. Engages in conduct aimed at making false representation of a student's academic performance; or
        6. Assists other students in any of these acts.

See UWS Ch. 14.03(2) for examples of academic misconduct

Investigation Process

If it appears that a student in your class may be guilty of academic misconduct, as defined by UWS 14.03, you must promptly ask the student to meet with you informally to discuss your concerns.*

1. Your request to meet with the student should indicate that you have questions about whether academic misconduct has occurred.

2. During this meeting, explain why you believe the student may have committed academic misconduct and share the evidence you have.

3. Remember this is an investigation and you should maintain an open mind. Give the student time during the meeting to respond and provide their perspective on the matter.

4. If you conclude that no misconduct occurred or that no penalty is warranted, this meeting will end the matter.

5. If you conclude that the student is guilty and that a penalty is warranted, you may choose from the following range of sanctions (See 'Sanctions'). You may impose more than one penalty.

6. If the semester is ending and grades are due when 1) you have not completed your investigation, or 2) before the student's 10 day period to request a hearing has expired, or 3) when a student has requested a hearing but it has not yet occurred, give the student an "I" (incomplete) until the matter is closed and final.

NOTE: Even if the recommended sanction is "removal from the course", students should **continue in class and take all exams** pending the decision of the hearing body.

If students not enrolled in your class are involved, or if you have reason to believe the student may have been involved in other incidents, or if you feel you could not give the student a fair hearing, you should contact the Dean of Students Office and ask for an Investigating Officer to be assigned to the case.

Sanctions

UWS Ch. 14.04(1) lists sanctions as "a" through "j." They are assembled by level of severity and procedural process as follows:

- Group A

    1. An oral reprimand

    2. A written reprimand presented only to the student

    3. An assignment to repeat the work, to be graded on its merits

- Group B

    4. A lower or failing grade on the particular assignment or test

    5. A lower grade in the course

    6. A failing grade in the course

    7. Removal of the student from the course in progress

    8. A written reprimand to be included in the student's disciplinary file

- Group C
    9. University disciplinary probation
    10.   Suspension or expulsion from the University

Procedures

UWS Ch. 14.05 & 14.06

Group A: Sanctions "a" through "c"

You can privately reprimand the student, either orally or in writing, and/or ask the student to repeat the work in which the misconduct occurred. Under the latter option, you must grade the work on its merits without making a deduction for the previous misconduct. No permanent record is made of the incident. The student does have the right to contest any penalty you impose, including the lower level sanctions. You must inform the student of the right to request a hearing within 10 days (See 'Students Right to a Hearing') and you should keep some notes about the incident.

Group B: Sanctions "d" through "h"

If you choose a sanction in this group, you must prepare a written report, (see example below) summarizing the reasons for your belief that misconduct occurred, proposing one or more sanctions, and notifying the student that he/she has the right to request a hearing within 10 days (See 'Students Right to a Hearing'). You must send or give a copy of your report to the student. Send a copy of the report to the Associate Dean of Students. The Associate Dean of Students may recommend an additional disciplinary sanction of probation or suspension if the student has committed academic misconduct more than once or if the student is in a professional or graduate program.

View sample letter to student

Group C: Sanctions "i" through "j"

If you conclude that disciplinary probation, suspension or expulsion is warranted, the incident must be referred to the Dean of Students Office. Your report to the Dean of Students Office should include a description of the incident and specification of the sanction recommended. Send or give a copy of this report to the student. The Investigating Officer will consult with you and will also meet with the student. A hearing will automatically be scheduled for these sanctions unless the student waives this right.

View sample letter to Associate Dean

*The _letter to student_ is used for sanctions "d" through "h" only, addressed to student and copy given to the Dean of Students Office. The _letter to the Associate Dean_ is used only for sanctions "i" through "j", is addressed to the Associate Dean, and a copy is given to the student.

- *The typical report is comprised of the following sections:*
  - **Explanation** *of the facts supporting instructor's conclusion*
  - **Disciplinary sanction** *being recommended*
  - **Notification** *of the student's right to a hearing*
  - **Notice** *of filing with the Associate Dean of Students*

The report may either be delivered to the student in person or be mailed to his/her current local address.

Student's Right to a Hearing

UWS Ch. 14.08

If the student wishes to contest any part of your report, he or she may request a hearing before the Student Disciplinary Hearing Committee. Requests must be made within 10 days of the instructor's oral or written decision. If the sanction you propose is probation, suspension, or expulsion from the University, the case will go to hearing automatically, unless the student waives this right. In cases where the recommended sanction is suspension or expulsion, the student may choose to have the hearing before either the Student Disciplinary Hearing Committee or before a single Hearing Officer designated by the Chancellor.
The instructor's role in the hearing will be that of a witness; you are not obliged to "prosecute" the case. At the hearing, the instructor, the Investigating Officer (if there is one), and the student will each be asked to present evidence and make a statement. The Student Disciplinary Hearing Committee or Hearing Officer will listen to the evidence and arguments and decide whether academic misconduct has occurred and what the appropriate sanction should be. The Student Disciplinary Hearing Committee or Hearing Officer is not limited to the sanction recommended by the instructor.
If the Student Disciplinary Hearing Committee or Hearing Officer prescribes suspension or expulsion, the student can appeal to the Chancellor, who will review the record of the case. Ordinarily, campus

decisions are final except that the Board of Regents may, at its discretion, grant a review of the record.

For More Information

For assistance with implementing the academic misconduct policies and procedures, please contact the staff of the Dean of Students Office at 715.232.1181 or email the Dean of Students Office at thomasj@uwstout.edu. To refer a case of academic misconduct to the Dean of Student Office, please contact the University's Judicial Officer, Joan Thomas, Associate Dean of Students.
Adapted from UW-Madison Dean of Students-Academic Misconduct Guide

Academic Dishonesty Defined

The Board of Regents, administrators, faculty, academic staff and students of the University of Wisconsin System believe that academic honesty and integrity are fundamental to the mission of higher education and to the University of Wisconsin System. The university has a responsibility to promote academic honesty and integrity and to develop procedures to deal effectively with instances of academic dishonesty. Students are responsible for the honest completion and representation of their work, for the appropriate citation of sources, and for respect of others' academic endeavors. Students who violate these standards must be confronted and must accept the consequences of their actions. Definitions of academic dishonesty as provided by the National Association of Student Personnel Administrators include:

Cheating intentionally

using or attempting to use unauthorized materials, information or study aids in any academic exercise.

Fabrication

intentional and unauthorized falsification or invention of any information or citation in an academic exercise.

Plagiarism

intentionally or knowingly representing the words or ideas of another as your own in any academic exercise. Plagiarism is considered a form of theft and is a serious violation at the university. Penalties can range from a lowered grade to expulsion.

Facilitating academic dishonesty intentionally or knowingly helping or attempting to help another to commit an act of academic dishonesty.

UW-Stout also considers academic dishonesty to include forgery of academic documents, or intentionally impeding or damaging the academic work of others.

A student charged with violation of academic policy will have a fair hearing. Academic misconduct in the University of Wisconsin System is defined by UWS Chapter 14.

Plagiarism Resources

Definition of plagiarism

According to the Honor Code at Wofford College (2006-2007), plagiarism is defined as:

1. the verbatim repetition, without acknowledgement, of the writings of another author
2. borrowing without acknowledging the source
3. paraphrasing the thoughts of another writer without acknowledgement
4. allowing any other person or organization to prepare work which one then submits as his/her own.

Remember, plagiarism is a concept and therefore a particular **act** may be defined differently by different people. **Each faculty member defines individual acts differently. Find out what your professor accepts as collaborative work and what he or she defines as plagiarism.**

Professor Clayton Whisnant has prepared a summary of issues related to plagiarism and the Wofford Honor Code called "**Living By the Wofford Honor Code.**"

Other types of academic dishonesty

The handbook defines other types of academic dishonesty.

1. Any conduct during an academic course which involves the unauthorized use of information obtained by any means.
2. The buying, selling, or theft of any assignment, examination, or quiz prior to its administration.
3. The unauthorized use of any electronic or mechanical device during any academic course.
4. The unauthorized collaboration on any test, assignment, or project.
5. Preparing any assignment for another to submit as his own.

The Internet

Information--including articles, illustrations, photographs, music, and video--are the intellectual property of the producer of the material. This may be the author or publisher.

However, in relation to your class, all materials obtained through the Internet have the same protection as any print material. **This means that all material you use, whether quoted verbatim or paraphrased, must be cited.** Find out from your professor which format he or she wishes for you to use. There are several sites on the web that provide guides for electronic citations.

Citation guides

NOTE: Print copies of all major style guides are available at the Reference Desk. The print version usually has a more complete description of what you need to do and why, and often covers special cases and sources that websites like the following do not.

General
Citing Sources--a list of resources prepared by Duke University libraries. Detailed examples of all major style guides (MLA, APA, Chicago, Turabian, etc.).

Electronic sources
University of Columbia Press--Provides examples and comparisons of citations in MLA, Chicago (Turbian) and APA forms.